To Dad

Merry Christmas (1997)

lovt n best wishes
Irene xx

GLORY, GLORY LIONS

The Taming Of South Africa

Chris Dighton
& Iain Spragg

GLORY, GLORY LIONS

By Chris Dighton
& Iain Spragg

Pictures by ALLSPORT/Alex Livesey & Dave Rogers

Allsport UK Ltd, 3, Greenlea Park, Prince George's Road, London SW19 2JD

Published by
Bookman Projects Limited
1 Canada Square, Canary Wharf, London E14 5AP

in association with
Hayters
146-148 Clerkenwell Road, London EC1R 5DP

First published 1997

ISBN 1840430052

Scanning and Image Quality by John Symonds

Contents

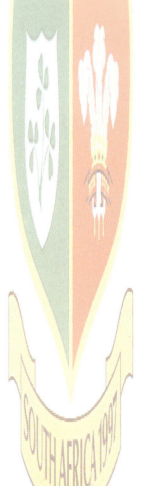

Cliff Morgan, OBE

The former Lion and most-capped Welsh fly-half

SCULPTURED in the mind and scorchingly realistic to those of us who watched them, the television pictures of a winning rugby adventure by the British and Irish rugby team in South Africa were visions of true greatness unfolding. We were deliriously happy in the reflected glory. The Lions of 97 reached horizons of spine-tingling skill and, with a breathtaking, robust, intelligent and healthy attitude, they shocked a whole nation that were World Cup winners and silenced a country gripped with rugby fever.

The performance of these Lions shattered the opinion that Southern Hemisphere rugby was light-years ahead of ours, as Martin Johnson's team laid down their winning cards, face upwards.

The supporters, who travelled with the team to the sun-drenched, rugby-crazy country, have been blessed with a perennial memory. They were all agog when the favourites and current World champions were beaten in a Test series.

This momentous victory is indelibly placed in rugby history and in the pages of this book which tell a remarkable tale with appealing simplicity.

When it was announced that Fran Cotton would be the team manager, it was realised that the former England and Lions prop forward, with that square jaw, was a no-nonsense man who would demand and inspire loyalty from his team. Cotton realised that he could stimulate the self-trust that is within all fine players with his sincerity and benevolence.

So he gathered around him the type of player that he knew would flourish on a difficult tour. He chose Martin Johnson – not the obvious selection – as captain because he knew, from experience, that Johnson could cope with the severity of the pressures and that he would be reliable and inspirational in the thick of the tough Springbok battles ahead.

Results confirm that unwavering faith, and Martin Johnson's name is now immortalised in the fabled book of rugby.

Then the coach, Ian McGeechan, a truly great centre in Scottish and Lions teams during his playing days, is a winner. His career is punctuated with innovation and a dedication to hard work and togetherness, for he is blessed with the gift of leadership – the trademark of his success.

His detailed analysis of the game is a startling example of how it should be played. He is an incomparable watchdog – constantly sniffing. Like Carwyn James, the Lions coach in New Zealand in 1971, he had the wit and wisdom to concentrate on fundamentals and encourage each person in the team to express himself, and not to ignore individual genius.

McGeechan also had the modesty to invite another mighty example of Scotland and Lions fame, Jim Telfer, to set the high and critical standards of forward play which proved to be crucial.

Just as in 1955 on the South African tour, it was the pack – the hard-working and selfless pack – who laid the foundations for victory, giving the talented and remarkable Irishman Tony O'Reilly enough ball to score a record number of tries on a Lions tour which still stands today. Life was easier for a player in those far-away days, Modern players are fitter and better prepared and more tactically aware. And they are professional and have to be committed and dedicated.

They have to be aware of all the things that go along with money. For instance the public expect so much, television demands a lot for its investment and so alters the pattern of fixtures – a non-stop round of Test matches, Sunday internationals and so on.

But that is part of the price of being a professional. It's not easy.

For instance, 44 years ago we were on tour for four months and played 25 games – not all tough – on the South African tour and so we had time to stop and stare and breathe. In contrast this year's Lions had 13 really tough games in just seven weeks, with little time for relaxation or rest from a constant battering of the body.

No Lions team in the past 100 years has faced such a task and, to their eternal credit, they took on the might of South African rugby – the crowds and the Press, too – with style and courage.

The quality of the play was stunning and they moved along with all the influences of

time. They never lost their composure and, more than anything else, their defensive class and their inspired togetherness makes them the greatest-ever Lions team.

Reading these pages you will not find stories of cliques and jealousies, but of heart-warming, genuine friendliness and togetherness in this extra special team.

There is the story of the back-room staff of doctors, physiotherapists, psychologists and press officers that augmented the top management. All so vital in the game today. We did not have a doctor or physio in 1955, neither did we have a coach – such were the laws and restrictions. On reflection it was amateur stuff and you begin to have misgivings.

I have not singled out any players, for that is done in the following pages. They were a team after all where togetherness was the key.

In the afterglow of this fabulous tour it is sad that administrators of the four Home Countries are still squabbling. Why don't they copy the management, the commitment and the fabulous understanding of the winning Lions of 1997?

For this was an expedition that made us all feel good in England, Scotland, Ireland and Wales.

Captain Courage

AS Martin Johnson led the lap of honour around Ellis Park, he wore the smile of a man who has proved his critics wrong. His selection as captain, his experience, his temperament, all had been questioned leading up to the Lions' tour of South Africa.

But here he was jogging around the pitch, a man-mountain of a player, surrounded by joyous team-mates and saluted by an admiring crowd. The last laugh is certainly loudest and in this case it not only echoed around the Johannesburg stadium, but reverberated throughout the rugby world.

British rugby was back on the map. In no small part due to the efforts of one Martin Osborne Johnson. And those who initially queried his appointment were unlikely to wish to be reminded of the fact as the Leicester and England lock led his side to a historic Test series achievement that not even a 35-16 defeat in the final match could tarnish. Wins in Cape Town and Durban had already ensured a series victory and, as captain, Johnson had secured his own place in the history books by being only the second man to lead a Lions tour to victory in South Africa this century.

It's been 23 years since Willie-John McBride's team managed the feat and few believed the team of 1997 could emulate the 1974 Lions. Faced with a Springboks team undefeated in their last seven games and champing at the bit to underline their credentials as world champions, Johnson had the task of leading the clear underdogs into hostile territory.

Before the trip, even he admitted: "I've not dared dream about winning the series in

South Africa. To do so as a player would be special, but as captain, it would be stupendous." McBride apart, only two men have previously headed home victorious – W E MacLagen in 1891, and Johnny Hammond in 1896.

The fact that we can now celebrate exactly that is a tribute to Johnson, who, through example and determination, led the Lions from the front and refused to buckle when the pressure was on. "My job in South Africa is to keep the whole party together, intent on a common purpose," he declared before the First Test. The degree to which he achieved that can be seen not only in the results, but in the team-spirit that he inspired throughout the squad.

"The feeling of unity and pride in each other has been a constant throughout," acknowledged centre Scott Gibbs. It was a pride that could be seen even in the midweek matches, when a British try would provoke as much celebration from the non-playing squad members as those on the pitch.

John Bentley admitted his over-riding memory from scoring a 70-metre solo effort against the Gauteng Lions was not the try itself but "the elation on the faces" of his colleagues watching.

That team spirit was to prove a valuable asset in the First Test in Cape Town. A match where the Lions had to fight for every ball, and endure some ferocious tackling, before Matt Dawson's superb solo try ensured victory.

"It's something you dream about," said a delighted Johnson afterwards. "Getting a win is great and we're on a real high now. The

standard of play we have produced has surprised a lot of people and there's been some tremendous stuff."

But, ever the captain, he didn't lose focus on the task ahead: "We've got a lot of hard work in front of us," he warned. "It's no good winning one Test and losing two. If we can win the second – which is a distinct possibility now – then we'll really have something to shout about."

However, with Johnson as skipper, plenty of people felt there was already something worth shouting about. Roger Uttley called him "a mountain of a man who has grown in stature since the tour began," while Bill Beaumont, the last Englishman to skipper a Lions team, simply stated: "Martin is the best front-jumper in the world." With the dream of winning the series becoming a truly attainable reality, the former Lions scrum-half Dewi Morris claimed Johnson was just "80 minutes from immortality".

Of course that would have been disputed by the Springboks, who were in no mood to be charitable following their defeat. If Cape Town had been tough, it was nothing compared to Durban where Johnson's men had to withstand an onslaught from a South African team hungry for revenge.

But with their backs to the wall, the Lions refused to buckle. The final 20 minutes saw not one British player stray offside, collapse a maul or lose his footing. Not one penalty was conceded in that final quarter nor one tackle shirked. Discipline was maintained and the reward was a second, decisive victory.

And now Johnson could celebrate. "No one gave us a chance before the tour, but we have proved a lot of people wrong. There has been an excellent team spirit displayed and some great characters and leaders on the tour."

Playing down his own contribution he remarked: "The captaincy is a little bit overplayed. Everyone played their part." It was a typical

understatement from a man who has always avoided hyperbole. Johnson has never been one to play the media game, although he would have been forgiven if he had wanted to settle a few personal scores. After all, only a few days before the Lions tour began, plenty of critics were still questioning the appointment of Johnson as captain. Here was a man, they said, who had never captained England, and had skippered only a handful of games at Leicester. In addition, they questioned his temperament, citing the incident only months earlier, in the England v Argentina game, when Johnson had punched an opponent just as Jeremy Guscott was about to score a try.

"That was a bad few minutes," admitted Johnson. "I could just see the headline: The punch that cost a try." Fortunately, England went on to win the game, but Johnson conceded: "That proved to be a valuable lesson. I knew then that I couldn't afford to do that for any side I played in, especially on a Lions tour, where all the games would be so tight."

A lesson learned, but the selectors had other considerations. Not since the war, had a player been appointed Lions skipper without first leading his country and even Johnson himself recognised "captain" was a pretty recent addition to his own CV. In the end, however, the decision came down to fairly simple criteria. As tour manager Fran Cotton said: "Johnson's was the first name you put on the team sheet and you need a captain who is guaranteed his place in the Test side." The significance of the appointment was obvious. By choosing the rough, tough 18-stone Johnson as captain, the Lions were clearly making a statement of intent for the tour. As Cotton admitted: "The selection is a business memo to the South Africans. When the captains are called for the toss, the giant shadow of a 'World XV' lock will fall across the home dressing room."

Fighting talk, but Johnson himself appeared more reserved: "The whole business of captaincy is pretty new to me," he said. "I did the job on an occasional basis with Leicester, as a stand in for Dean Richards to begin with. But playing in the second row means it can be difficult to control the whole game. Even so, it was a huge honour and a bit of a shock when Fran told me on the phone."

But Cotton recognised in Johnson more than just a hulking figure who could terrify opponents. He saw also a man who would not buckle when the going got tough. "I asked two questions at the end," said Cotton. "How is this player going to cope with severe pressure, and is he going to be on the front foot or the back foot? Character was a vital part of the selection process. And Martin fitted the bill."

Events have proved Cotton right, which will come as no surprise to anyone who has followed Johnson's career. He seems to have made a habit of swimming comfortably when thrown in at the deep end.

Nonetheless, it is a measure of the man that he rose to the challenge, leading the Lions to their first series win in South Africa since 1974 and in the process restoring a confidence in the team not witnessed since the tour of Australia in the late 80's.

It is a feat that assures Johnson a place in the game's history and he has risen to every challenge that has come his way, including captaincy.

"I don't enjoy that part of the job to be honest," he admits. "I always seem to get asked the same questions. And while I know the Press boys have a job to do, I can sometimes get a little impatient. Some people take a lot for granted."

The Lions captain who, when not leading teams to historic victories, works part-time for a bank, enjoys sports trivia and admits to not smiling much. He claims he is "the most boring man in rugby".

Nonetheless, he is fast becoming one of the most talked about players in the game. His triumphant captaincy in South Africa was just the latest milestone in a career that has seen him described as the greatest lock in the world and earned him the first £1 million deal in British Rugby Union. Former Leicester scrum-half, Darren Grewcock, who now runs The Sports Connection, a promotional company that lists Johnson among

its clients, says: "A few players, like Will Carling, have made money out of marketing and promotion, but Martin is now in a position to be the first to make a million from playing the game. And why not? I would say he is the most valuable player in the world – but then, I'm biased!"

The plaudits were justified, but disguised the fact that Johnson has served a long apprenticeship in the game. His baptism in international rugby is a perfect example. A regular in the Leicester side, Johnson had gained England 'B' caps against France and Italy in 1992, but the 22-year-old believed that a full cap was still some way off when he was summoned to Twickenham in March 1993 as cover for Wade Dooley. When Dooley pulled out of the Five Nations' match with France, Johnson stepped on to the international stage with the confidence of a veteran, acquitting himself with honours in a 16-15 victory. In fact, when England – without Johnson – subsequently lost to Wales and Ireland, Geoff Cooke, then England manager, confessed: "On balance, I probably regret not persisting with him for the rest of the winter."

The following summer, Johnson proved his England performance had been no fluke. This time Dooley pulled out of the Lions' tour to New Zealand and Johnson, on tour with England 'A' in Canada, suddenly found himself flying to the other side of the world to join the team.

From Vancouver to Christchurch, via Toronto and Heathrow, Johnson spent nearly two and a half days perched some 30,000 feet in the air, but there were no signs of jet lag when he got on the rugby pitch.

After two outstanding performances against the provincial sides of Taranaki and Auckland, Johnson was thrust into the cauldron of a Wellington Test match against the All Blacks. The Lions won 20-7 and the Leicester lock was on his way.

It was a far cry from the furniture-smashing antics of his youth. Back then, the Johnson household would reverberate to the sound of Martin and his younger brother Will clattering into the dining-room table as they practised their scrummaging.

Fortunately, mother Hilary is a PE teacher and therefore perhaps slightly more forgiving than some would have been with the indoor sports activity. She is also a dedicated runner who has competed in marathons in London, New York and Paris, and could appreciate the lengths her son would go to in order to fulfil his sporting desires.

Which is fortunate because Johnson lives and breathes rugby. When he's not playing, he's training. If he's not training, he's watching videos of opponents to gauge their strengths and weaknesses. For relaxation, he has been known to challenge others to answer sports trivia questions and even his first big break in the game came while he was supposed to be on holiday.

After leaving school in Market Harborough in 1980, he journeyed to New Zealand for an extended sojourn in King Country, North Island. The local club there, College Old Boys, found themselves short of locks and recruited the young, but already 6' 8'' Johnson.

King Country's chairman was the former All Black, Colin Meads, whose tutelage of the young Johnson culminated in a call-up to the New Zealand Under-21 side alongside Blair Larsen, John Timu and Va'aiga Tuigamala – all of whom went on to play for the All-Blacks.

Indeed, Meads believes Johnson too would have become a full international if he had remained in New Zealand. However, after an 18-month stay (extended from 12 months due to a recurring shoulder injury), Johnson returned to England in 1991 to work as a banker in Market Harborough and try to establish himself in the Leicester team.

Chosen for a third-team match against Moseley, he quickly made an impression. Especially when one of the opposition players made the mistake of trying to test his mettle with a series of dirty tricks, from straying elbows to misplaced fists.

After one stray punch too many, Johnson turned, delivered a useful right-hander of his own, and then calmly asked whether they could now get on with playing rugby.

His senior debut for Leicester was almost as dramatic. Injuries to both the club's first choice locks ensured a late call up for the Pilkington Cup game against Bath. But as the West Country giants had comfortably won 9-3 on their visit the previous week, few held out much hope for the trip to The Rec. As usual however, Johnson wasn't fazed. He played an absolute blinder and the Tigers came away with a 12-0 victory.

A series of fine performances for Leicester followed and Johnson was soon a first-team regular.

But as his reputation grew, he refused to get carried away with his success at Welford Road, insisting : "It's a team game. The Press start telling you what a magnificent match you've had, but it's the combined efforts of all the lads that bring you the results. We spend a lot of

time working on the teamwork of it. People can praise me and tell me what a wonderful game I've had but others have to play well too." Nonetheless, he continued to attract attention. By 1994, he had become an England regular and was a key figure in the World Cup campaign. His reading of the game was second to none and the sheer consistency of his performances slowly turned his contribution to the international team from important to indispensable.

By 1996, Will Carling's successor had become a topic of regular discussion and many were predicting Johnson would be in the frame. His club captain at Leicester, Dean Richards, was one of the many who supported the idea. "He is an instinctive rugby player," insisted Richards, "and his leadership skills are coming out as he matures as a person."

A trait recognised by Leicester when they named Johnson as the first-team captain – a role he has handled with aplomb although, as usual, he plays down his own contribution .

"I have my say at Leicester," acknowledges Johnson, "but I'm lucky. The club is an exceptionally well-run outfit with the best stadium in the country and men who have done it all, like Paul Dodge and Peter Wheeler, who value input from the players who now have to go out and do it.

"And we already have a set of routines in terms of what we do before games, how we warm up, so as captain I just try to make sure that the mood of the team is right. If things are slack, I ensure that players buck their ideas up and if they are nervous, I try to relax them."

It sounds simple, but it was enough to get him the captain's job for the trip to South Africa. The call was duly made, but Johnson had little time to celebrate on hearing the news. "Leicester were playing Wasps the next day," he explained, "so I was too busy preparing for that to open the bottles of champagne.

"In fact, because of a pile up of fixture towards the end of the season, I didn't get a chance to celebrate at all. The thought of winning a Test series in South Africa as a player is special. But as captain it is stupendous." Now does that sound like a boring guy to you?

Aubrey Ganguly

The Challenge Ahead

THERE is nothing like an impending British Lions tour to add spice to the domestic rugby season: who will be selected, how will the team fare? Such questions dominate talk. Suddenly run-of-the-mill league fixtures become crucial head-to-head clashes between potential rivals for a place and there is an extra sparkle to the Five Nations as the Lions management pore over the cream of British talent.

The excitement comes to a head as selection day approaches and every self-proclaimed bar-room philosopher and the most respected reporters and columnists have their say.

First on the agenda for the epic 1997 tour to South Africa was the choice of management – and the Lions had a triumvirate of men who boasted a wealth of experience between them – Fran Cotton, Ian McGeechan and Jim Telfer.

Cotton, a veteran of three Lions tours, including the historic series win over the Springboks in 1974, was well aware of the unique demands South Africa presented. Universally respected within the game as a straight talker, he was charged as manager with moulding a disparate group of British players into a squad capable of toppling the reigning World Cup holders.

The Home Unions' Touring Committee appointed Ian McGeechan as head coach. The Northampton Director of Rugby boasted an enviable record of success and his appointment made him the first man to coach three successive Lions' parties. A veteran of eight Lions Tests, McGeechan guided

Scotland to their famous Grand Slam triumph in 1990 after coaching the 1989 Lions to a 2-1 series victory in Australia.

To complete the set, Jim Telfer, the Scottish Rugby Union Director of Coaching, was asked to take charge of the forwards. The son of a Borders' shepherd, Telfer also had Lions blood coursing through his veins having toured twice as a player to Australia and New Zealand in 1966 and South Africa in 1968. He was the coach for the 1993 tour to New Zealand.

There were no complaints with the management who were determined to do things their way as Cotton soon demonstrated when he announced a break with tradition – the 1997 squad would be extended from the conventional 30 players to 35. It was a lesson learned from the All Blacks who had taken 36 men to South Africa in 1996 and as a consequence recorded their first series win over the Springboks on their own soil.

"It is essential we are able to field sides of Test Match strength throughout the tour," Cotton said. "Our plan is to take two full teams plus additional players in key positions such as hooker, prop, centre and scrum-half."

With the management team in place and the size of the squad settled, thoughts turned to

the 64-thousand-dollar question: who would actually be on the plane that left for South Africa in May? In many ways Cotton, McGeechan and Telfer were spoiled for choice and helped by a first season of professional rugby in Britain which had raised general fitness levels to a new high – essential for a seven-week trek in hostile rugby country. The selection process got serious in February 1996 when they announced a 62-man provisional squad which immediately put the cat among the pigeons. A heavy reliance on Englishmen was inevitable – 27 players compared to the 13 each from Ireland and Wales and just nine Scots. But the main talking point was an apparent snub of the England three-quarters.

Jack Rowell's side had demolished Scotland and Ireland with a record flurry of points in their 1997 Five Nations clashes, yet Cotton and Co had overlooked the England skipper Phil de Glanville as well as excluding wingers Jon Sleightholme and Tony Underwood – generally regarded as the two most clinical finishers in the tournament. In their place were names which

surprised rugby followers and dumbfounded everybody else.

In came Jim Mallinder, Sale's uncapped full-back, Denis Hickie, Ireland's relatively untried winger and Martin Corry, the Bristol captain yet to make his full international debut. Also included were Leicester's Will Greenwood, Watsonians' Tom Smith and Bristol's David Corkery – all relatively inexperienced at the highest level. Six former rugby league players were also included – John Bentley, Dai Young, Scott Gibbs, Allan Bateman, Scott Quinnell and Alan Tait. That decision proved inspired as Bentley, Gibbs and Tait all made the Test side on merit and confounded those who thought they could not perform at such a level after so long out of the union game.

Cotton manfully defended the unorthodox selection: "We're looking for players who can do certain things and we've a different philosophy from many of the national managers on how to beat South Africa. There's still time for players to force their

way in. It's up to those left out to confirm or improve to fit in with our philosophy of playing rugby against the Springboks. A lot of players have been omitted and in the case of de Glanville it is clear that we have a fantastic amount of talent in the centre."

For perhaps the first time, the Lions management were picking a squad specifically tailored to the unique demands of a tour to South Africa. For decades the Springboks had hammered their opponents into submission with fearsome forward power and few sides have ever emerged from such a bloody war of attrition with a victory, let alone a series win.

As Cotton added: "Size is always important in international rugby, but even more so out there... only the tough need pack their suitcases."

THE SQUAD (pictured above):

Back row: Allan Bateman (Richmond & Wales), Mark Regan (Bristol & England), Robert Howley (Cardiff & Wales), Neil Jenkins (Pontypridd & Wales), Barry Williams (Richmond & Wales), Paul Grayson (Northampton & England), Nick Beal (Northampton & England), Tim Stimpson (Newcastle & England), John Bentley (Newcastle & England), Tom Smith (Watsonians & Scotland), Gregor Townsend (Northampton & Scotland), Paul Wallace (Saracens & Ireland), Neil Back (Leicester & England), Austin Healey (Leicester & England), Andy Keast (Coaching Assistant).

Middle row: Stan Bagshaw (Baggage master), Alan Tait (Newcastle & Scotland), Keith Wood (NEC Harlequins & Ireland), Scott Quinnell (Richmond & Wales), Will Greenwood (Leicester), Jeremy Davidson (London Irish & Ireland), Simon Shaw (Bristol & England), Doddie Weir

(Newcastle & Scotland), Tim Rodber (Northampton, Army & England), Lawrence Dallaglio (Wasps & England), Richard Hill (Saracens & England), Graham Rowntree (Leicester & England), Matt Dawson (Northampton & England), Mark Davies (Physio-therapist), Bob Burrows (Media Liaison Officer), Richard Wegrzyk (Masseur).

Front row: Samantha Peters (Administrative Assistant), Dr James Robson (Medical officer), Jason Leonard (NEC Harlequins & England), Dai Young (Cardiff & Wales), Ieuan Evans (Llanelli & Wales) Dave McLean (Fitness Advisor), Fran Cotton (Team manager), Martin Johnson (Leicester & England, captain), Ian McGeechan (Head coach), Jim Telfer (Assistant coach), Jeremy Guscott (Bath & England), Rob Wainwright (Watsonians & Scotland), Tony Underwood (Newcastle & England), Scott Gibbs (Swansea & Wales), Dave Aldred (Kicking coach)

Within days of this announcement of the squad, however, the inevitable squabbling and repercussions had begun. De Glanville used an appearance at Cambridge University as a platform to attack Cotton, inferring that he had been left out because of personal differences between the two men. There was also a fierce debate about the captaincy issue. The provisional squad lacked an obvious candidate. The problem lay in the fact that the players who had experience of leading an international side – Rob Wainwright, Ieuan Evans, Jonathan Humphreys and Jim Staples – could not be certain of a place in the Lions' first-choice line-up. The effect of the early selection was soon felt throughout the domestic game – Alan Tait was suddenly recalled to the Scotland side to face Ireland, nine years after he won his last cap.

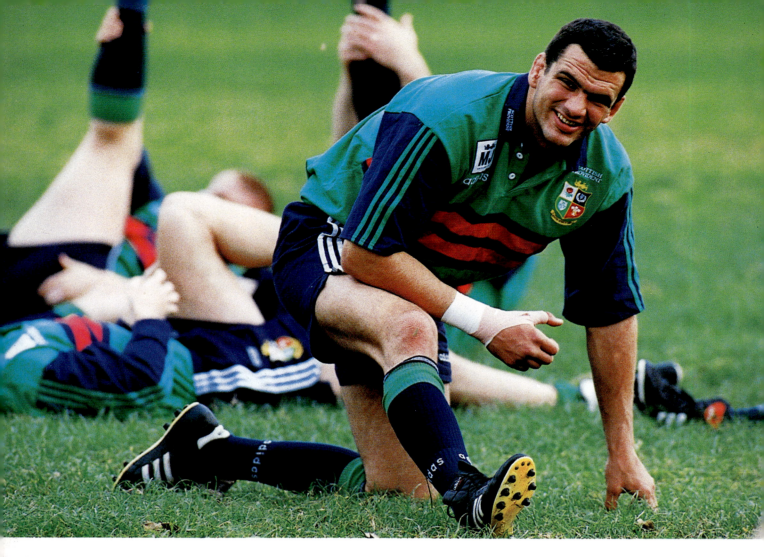

Number 8 Eric Miller, another surprise choice who had replaced the inimitable Dean Richards in the Leicester first team, also made the Ireland team. Attention also focused on injuries as players battled to either regain fitness or stay fit long enough to make the final squad – the big worries were the Ireland pair Simon Geoghegan and Keith Wood, both nursing long-term injuries. Wood, favourite to wear the No 2 shirt in the Tests, had dislocated his shoulder against France in the January and had undergone surgery to repair the damage. Geoghegan's prospects were bleaker. An ankle injury meant the flying Bath winger had made just two appearances for his club all season.

In March the 62 became 35 and Cotton, McGeechan and Telfer had some more surprises up their sleeve. The biggest shocks were the inclusion of Neil Back, Tony Underwood, Peter Clohessy and Barry Williams, all of whom had been initially excluded. Clohessy was perhaps the luckiest of all to be selected considering his chequered past. The fiery Irish prop, nicknamed 'The Claw', had been banned from international rugby for six months for stamping on French lock Olivier Roumat in 1996 and had since moved to Queensland to play in the Super-12s. But the Lions needed players who would not flinch

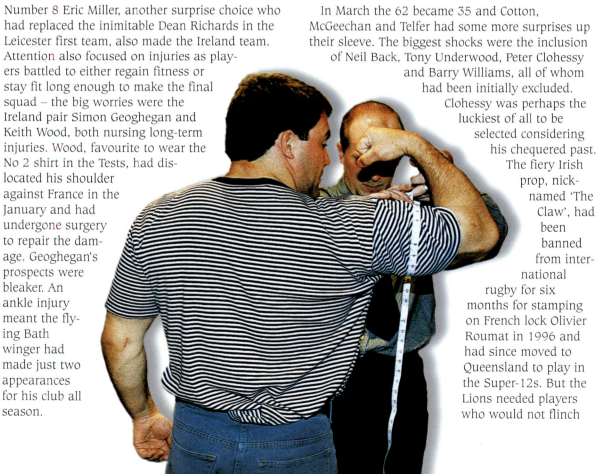

When the Lions run onto the field there is a sense of anticipation about them being there. For eight weeks we are part of South Africa. We must be part of that environment
— Ian McGeechan

when the South Africans started playing hard and after a phone call to Queensland coach Don Connolly, Clohessy was given the nod.

Another surprise selection was Barry Williams, the 22-year-old Neath hooker who was Wales' third choice No 2 and had been capped just once. He leap-frogged Humphreys and Swansea's Garin Jenkins to earn his place.

The announcement also settled the captaincy issue – Leicester's Martin Johnson becoming only the second Englishmen since the war to be given the honour. It was another gamble that worked. Johnson was not even the Leicester club captain although he had led the side in the absence of Dean Richards. In many ways the decision was as much a statement of intent to the Springboks as it was forced upon the committee. "Martin has got total respect from his own team and, just as importantly, the opposition," Cotton said.

"That's a hell of a start when you are new to captaincy. He will be the focal point of the side, involved at the sharp end from start to finish." The new captain said: "It's going to be more physical than anything we are used to in Five Nations. The South Africans will try to intimidate us in a fair way. It can be very physical out there, without being dirty. We have just got to stand up to it. There are guys in the squad like Ieuan Evans, Jason Leonard and Rob Wainwright who captained their country so I will rely heavily on their experience."

This was an aggressive, combative squad. The choice of Wales prop Dai Young, England hooker Mark Regan and Newcastle winger John Bentley all smacked of matching fire with fire. Nor were men like Scott Gibbs, Tim Stimpson and Jeremy Davidson going to be overawed by the time-honoured myth of South African rugby, found by many to be the real thing.

The soft spot appeared to be the kicking department where the selection seemed to put an over-reliance on Neil Jenkins. Without Wales' record points-scorer, the Lions looked susceptible and had only picked one other recognised kicker in Paul Grayson. The Northampton and England fly-half had been out of action since March when he damaged his hip in the League action and if he had broken down the Lions would have had to turn to Tim Stimpson – not even the first-choice kicker at his club Newcastle. The weeks ticked down

It's a long stretch whichever way you look at it for Martin Johnson (facing page, top), and Rob Howley and Neil Back (above) – and especially for the Lions' tailor as he tries to find something fitting for giant prop Jason Leonard

and there was encouraging news from South London where Keith Wood made a stunning return to the Harlequins side after his shoulder problems.

The Ireland hooker scored two tries in a victory over Bristol to confirm he was back to form and fitness, he was rarin' to go. The only pre-tour casualty was Peter Clohessy, who broke down with a back problem when the Lions met up days before their flight. However, one

The Lions will be no push-overs, as Neil Back (main pic) shows. The squad had a state-of-the-art scrummaging machine to help sharpen their skills. Lawrence Dallaglio (facing page) signals how many Tests he thinks they'll win, while Tony Underwood looks as though he's joined the cast of Gladiators in his protective body armour

Irishman's misfortune was another's gain as Cotton turned to Saracens' Paul Wallace to fill the gap. So the talking was over, the 1997 British Lions, kitted and booted, were assembled and ready for what was to be the biggest challenge of their careers. Could they become only the third side this century to win a series in South Africa?

We would all find out soon enough...

The Challenge Ahead

The Provincial Games

WHILE any touring side will ultimately be judged on its Test match record, the performance in the provincial games creates the foundations and sets the tone for the tour. If the team plays well and wins, confidence soars, generating a sense of belief vital to any campaign away from home.

If, however, the provincial games go badly the tour can be derailed. Look no further than the previous two Lions tours; to Australia in 1989 and New Zealand four years later. In Australia they won all the provincial games which gave the squad the mental edge to bounce back after losing the First Test in Sydney and triumph in the last two, clinching the series.

Four years later, in New Zealand, the Lions lost four of their 10 non-internationals, the squad became polarised and the first choice XV were crushed 30-13 in the all-important Third Test in Auckland, losing the series 2-1.

The provincial games on any Lions tour are invaluable in shaping the Test team. Every squad departs with a mix of recognised stars and promising youngsters and it is only through the action in the early matches that the selectors can assess their players and find the elusive right blend.

This was never better illustrated than in South Africa where Paul Wallace, Tom Smith, Jeremy Davidson and Alan Tait originally seemed destined to watch the Tests from the comfort of the stands but forced their way into contention with outstanding performances in the provincial matches.

Eastern Province XV 11
British Lions 39
May 24, Port Elizabeth

The 1997 Lions went into their first match of the tour against Eastern Province in Port Elizabeth desperate to announce their arrival with a victory. Only Ieuan Evans, Jason Leonard and Jeremy Guscott had toured with the Lions before and it was vital they guided the rest through what was always going to be a tough match against the traditionally aggressive Eastern Province side.

A confidence-boosting victory was essential and the Lions delivered, winning 39-11, running in five tries and, perhaps more importantly, conceding just one. In front of the 25,000-strong crowd in the sun-drenched Boet Erasmus Stadium, the visitors quickly found their

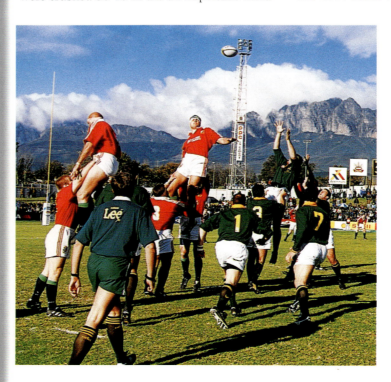

Ian McGeechan expounds his theories at a Lions training session (right) ... Jason Leonard (right) and his team put them to the test in the opening victory against Eastern Province at Port Elizabeth

rhythm. The Wales No 8 Scott Quinnell found the hard ground very much to his liking and, manfully supported by England flankers Lawrence Dallaglio and Richard Hill, helped steady any nerves the young Lions may have had.

Neil Jenkins was also at his reliable best and his calming influence from full-back was a major bonus. Wales' record points-scorer converted all five of the Lions tries by Guscott (2), Greenwood, Underwood and Weir, and landed two penalties. The only blot on the copybook came 10 minutes after the break when South Africa 'A' winger Deon Kayser crashed over for a try to give Eastern Province an unexpected 11-10 lead. Suddenly the Lions were presented with the first crisis of the tour, but they responded brilliantly, running in four tries in a 17-minute second-half burst.

There were many plus points from the game, notably the understanding Quinnell, Hill and Dallaglio struck up in the backrow, but the kicking from hand of Gregor Townsend – already pencilled in for the Test matches – must have worried the management of Fran Cotton, Ian McGeechan and Jim Telfer. Free from injury and buoyed by a satisfactory opening win, the squad moved east along the coast to face Border and even at this stage it was clear that the attitude of the 35-man squad was markedly different from the 1993 tour to New Zealand, which had degenerated into a counter-productive 'them and us' situation.

The more collective approach of the 1997 British Lions was in part due to the man-management of Cotton and skipper Martin Johnson, but also because the Test side was far from set in stone – places were up for grabs. Everybody realised the elusive dream of winning a Lions cap was within reach if they performed well.

This was most graphically illustrated by the fight between rival hookers Mark Regan and Barry Williams during training. The brief fracas, amicably resolved on the bus back to the hotel, showed the depth of commitment and passion engendered in the squad.

Border 14
British Lions 18
May 28, East London

As a squad the Lions were still finding their feet and adjusting to South Africa's vastly contrasting conditions which were starkly evident from the moment they arrived in East London.

While the match in Port Elizabeth had been played in glorious sunshine on a firm ground, the pitch of the Basil Kenyon Stadium in East London had been subjected to 36 hours of rain which had turned it into a mud bath.

The slippery conditions should have suited the northern hemisphere visitors better than Border, but the Lions conspired to make so many mistakes that, at one point, defeat – which would have been their first against a South African province since 1968 – looked more probable than possible.

Ironically the match started with a flurry of inventive and attacking Lions rugby which culminated with a try after two minutes for Newcastle's John Bentley who rounded off a sweeping move which saw the ball shifted through many hands, Tim Stimpson providing the decisive pass.

With the cushion of an early score the Lions should have relaxed against one of South Africa's weakest Provinces, but they tried to force the pace when the conditions dictated a slow, forward-dominated approach. Time and again the ball was spilled, choking the Lions' attacking intentions. When they did apply the basics of 'wet-weather' rugby they enjoyed more success and scored a second try through hooker Mark Regan after Eric

Miller, who had a highly impressive debut in a Lions' shirt, had picked up from the base of the scrum.

Nerves began to fray, however, when on the stroke of half-time, Border winger Andre Classen was sent over in the corner. Then just after the break fly-half Greg Miller landed his third penalty of the afternoon to leave the Lions trailing 14-10. To their credit, and despite their lack of matches together, the team did not panic even though conditions under foot were deteriorating.

They reverted to a tight, disciplined game as they tried to claw their way back and there were audible sighs of relief when acting-skipper Rob Wainwright crossed for the decisive try seven minutes from time. Scotland's Doddie Weir gathered the ball from an attacking line-out and was driven on by his pack, the Scotland captain charging through a tangle of bodies for the try. Tim Stimpson, who assumed the kicking duties after Paul Grayson missed five from five, added an injury-time penalty.

McGeechan, the Lions' coach, admitted it had been a tricky encounter, but was pleased with the result. "You are starting from scratch with a new set of players, yet the excitement of the tour opening has passed," he said.

"It was the worst possible conditions you could choose to put out a new side in, but it was encouraging that we gained more control in the second half."

On the negative side, however, there were already worries about key members of the squad. Scott Gibbs was flown to a Cape Town hospital for an X-ray on his left ankle, while Grayson was clearly struggling for form and had not quite shaken off the hip injury which cut short his domestic season.

Unbeaten, but not wholly convincing in their first two games, the Lions travelled to Cape Town for their clash with Western Province, one of the top-dogs in South African rugby.

The mood in the squad was still positive, but reports

Airborne: Rob Wainwright finishes with a flourish as he racks up a hat-trick of tries against Mpumalanga

in the South African press about the Lions inability to dominate a poor Border side did not go unnoticed. The first serious question about the strength of the squad had been asked.

The selectors, however, were in a position to begin experimenting with possible combinations for the Tests and only by giving the players freedom on the pitch could they hope to find a side capable of beating the World Cup holders.

Western Province 21
British Lions 38
May 31, Cape Town

Led for the first time by tour captain Johnson, the Lions scored four well-worked tries through Bentley (2), Evans and Alan Tait, but failed to look entirely convincing for the whole 80 minutes. The victory was comfortable enough, but they conceded three tries and struggled in the front row contest where the England pairing of Leonard and Graham Rowntree had a torrid afternoon.

Pre-tour it had been accepted that the Lions would opt for a predominantly, if not wholly, English front five for the Test matches, but Leonard and Rowntree's inability to come to terms with the Western Province scrummaging set alarm bells ringing.

One English Lion who did emerge with credit from the game was Tim Stimpson who added considerable weight to his claims as a regular kicker with seven out of eight attempts at goal for 18 points. The pick of the Lions' tries was by Evans, which came courtesy of a searing break by Welsh wizard Robert Howley – living up to his billing as the most complete scrum-half in the Northern Hemisphere.

However, the highlight of the match was undoubtedly the on-going clash between Bentley and James Small. Both men are known for never shirking a challenge and they lived up to expectations in front of 45,000 fans in the Newlands Stadium when Small took exception to the way he was bundled into touch by the abrasive Newcastle winger, followed up by claims that Bentley was guilty of eye-gouging.

More significant, in terms of the first Test match, was the way Bentley got the better of his much-vaunted opponent, scoring two tries and shutting out Small. The eye-gouging claims were strongly refuted. If they were buoyed by their latest win, the Lions were soon brought down to earth when it became clear Grayson would play no further part in the tour because of his persistent hip problems. Bath's versatile Mike Catt was summoned from England's tour in Argentina.

The Lions management were also concerned about the scrummaging frailties which had been exposed by Western Province. Realising their entire game plan became redundant if they could not provide even a semblance of a forward platform, the Lions set to work. Telfer called an extra scrummaging session to sort the problem and after an intensive session in the blistering sun, he was content that there would be no repeat of the Western Province debâcle.

"That session was as tough as you'll ever get, considering the hot conditions. We put in 46 scrums in 42 minutes but it was all absolutely necessary if we are to succeed," Telfer said.

By now the side to play in the First Test was beginning to take shape in the minds of the rugby public back home if not in the management's reckoning.

The main areas of contention were in the front five and at wing where Tait, Bentley, Evans and Underwood had all made strong cases for inclusion. Bentley had already scored three tries and Evans, the senior citizen of the squad at 33, looked as sharp and hungry as ever.

Mpumalanga 14
British Lions 64
June 3, Witbank

Mpumalanga, formerly known as South East Transvaal, had taken some notable senior scalps in South Africa's 1996 Currie Cup competition before losing to Orange Free State in the quarter-finals.

And with the benefit of hindsight this game was something of a watershed for the Lions – their comprehensive 64-14 demolition of the home side made South Africans sit up and take notice because it was achieved with such style. The Lions scored 10 tries in a scintillating display which included a quick-fire hat-trick

by Wainwright in a record nine minutes. Tony Underwood and Evans scored two apiece with Matt Dawson, Jenkins and Nick Beal also touching down.

Some of the rugby played was breath-taking and far, far removed from the often tedious, over-cautious approach witnessed in some Five Nations campaigns. It seemed the British and Irish game was catching up with the southern hemisphere.

However the celebrations were muted when the darker side of South African rugby surfaced. Weir's knee was the target of a savage and unprovoked kick from the Mpumalanga lock Marius Bosman at a ruck.

Bosman's assault left Weir with serious medial ligament damage and forced him out of the tour. Wainwright escaped with just bruises from a vicious raking by Elandre van den Bergs.

Cotton was furious and, after reviewing the video, launched a blistering attack on Mpumalanga and Bosman particularly.

"Everybody will understand there are enormous legal implications if the local union do not take appropriate action," he said.

"My priority is to ensure that the Lions are properly protected by the referee. It is a hard enough game as it is without gratuitous violence which has tragically ended Doddie Weir's tour."

Northern Transvaal 35
British Lions 30

June 7, Pretoria

If the loss of Weir was not bad enough, the Lions now faced the daunting task of tackling Northern Transvaal – one of South Africa's strongest Provinces – at the intimidating Loftus Versveld stadium. The 'Blue Bulls' boasted an array of talent in their line-up and had reached the semi-finals of the 1996 Super-12 where they lost to eventual champions Auckland. This was the blot on the Lions' copybook but not a huge surprise. More

James Small refuses John Bentley's hand at the end of the Western Province game, as their feud rumbled on. Rob Howley (facing page) enhanced his reputation as the best scrum-half in the Northern game in the 38-21 victory

alarming for Cotton, McGeechan and Telfer was the manner in which they lost. The Lions pack failed throughout to come to terms with their Northern Transvaal counterparts and struggled for parity in both the scrums and line-outs.

This was South African power rugby and the tourists had been found wanting. The home side dominated the first-half and established an 18-7 half-time lead with tries from Danie van Schalkwyk and fly-half Steyn as the slightly ponderous Lions team struggled to stay with the pace. After the break they emphasised their superiority with a try by captain Adriaan Richter just minutes after the restart. The Lions clawed their way back into contention with tries from Townsend and Guscott, his second of the match, but their revival was nipped in the bud when a Townsend pass was intercepted by van Schalkwyk for Northern Transvaal's side's fourth try.

Despite a late flurry and no little adventure, Johnson's men could not cut the deficit and the Lions had lost their first match against a provincial side in South Africa for 29 years. Further bad news followed when Gibbs was cited for a punch on a Northern Transvaal player which had gone unnoticed by the referee. The Welshman was banned for one match.

To add insult to injury Quinnell was forced out of the tour with a groin injury which needed immediate treatment and rest back home. Bruised but far from bowed the Lions headed south for the sixth match of the tour against Gauteng Lions – a powerful side which had beaten the touring England team by three points in 1994.

With the First Test ten days away, competition for places was becoming even more intense and some surprising candidates for full recognition had surfaced at the expense of more seasoned internationals. In the front row few fans would have bet against Leonard making the Test side and adding to the two caps he won in New Zealand in 1993, but suddenly he found himself under pressure from the unheralded Wallace and Smith.

Also pressing hard was the Ireland No 8 Miller, the youngest player in the Lions' squad. His dynamic play and extra pace seeming to suit the management's grand scheme better than the more conventional Rodber.

With a shake of the hips, Matt Dawson eludes his tackler to score against Mpumalanga. But (facing page) the Lions show their disappointment at defeat by Northern Transvaal

John Bentley leaves the Gauteng cover trailing in his wake while (opposite) Tim Rodber punches a hole in the defence. Scott Quinnell (below right) ponders the meaning of life...

Gauteng Lions 14
British Lions 20

June 11, Johannesburg

Victory against Gauteng was vital to restore the momentum of the tour and, courtesy of some inspired defence and clinical finishing, this was exactly what the Lions delivered in a dramatic 20-14 triumph.

However the match will be best remembered for a moment of sublime vision and execution from John Bentley rather than for saving a tour which could have degenerated into disaster.

Receiving the ball from Neil Jenkins a full 70 metres from the Gauteng line, Bentley looked up

briefly to assess his options, but either didn't see or care about the mass of defenders baring down on him. Instead of taking a tackle to set up a ruck, looking for touch or any other conventional solution to his predicament, Bentley set off on a run which took him past or through seven tacklers on his way to scoring beneath the posts.

It was a glorious individual effort which galvanised his team-mates and they wrapped up the match five minutes later when Austin Healey scampered over. After the game Bentley put his sensational score into perspective.

"I was poor on Saturday against Northern Transvaal when I was substituted and had been down since then," he said. "Sometimes you have got to shut up and put up and it was up to me to respond in the best possible fashion. I am very pleased," he added.

His manager Fran Cotton was a little more enthusiastic about the try when asked how important it was to the Lions as a whole. "There is often a defining moment on a tour and this without doubt was a tremendous success," he said.

With just two games left against Natal, the reigning Currie Cup holders, and an Emerging Springboks side, the Lions were beginning to take shape and many critics were now more optimistic about their chances in the three-match series.

This revision of opinion was due in large part to the sense of unity between the players which emerged through the tour and made nonsense of the idea that a Lions squad consisted of a first-choice XV and the mid-week side, known as the 'dirt-trackers'.

The competition for places only served to foster a greater team spirit rather than fragment the players and there were no signs of the nationalist splits which had blighted the 1993 Lions in New Zealand.

Traditionally the closer the Lions get to their first international the easier it is to pick the Test side. What made the 1997 Lions squad different was that the nearer the Cape Town clash got, the harder it became for Cotton and McGeechan to settle on their best line-up.

Neil Back's performances made Richard Hill far from an automatic choice at open-side, Alan Bateman was pushing Guscott and Gibbs as if his life depended on it and Tim Stimpson had silenced his doubters with some fine kicking displays as well as showing his customary incisive, forceful running.

At this point of the tour the Lions had already silenced some of the more sceptical South African critics, but doubts persisted about the side when it was confronted by the full Springbok team.

In a break from tradition, the Springbok selectors had decided to exclude their top players from the Provincial games in preparation for the Test

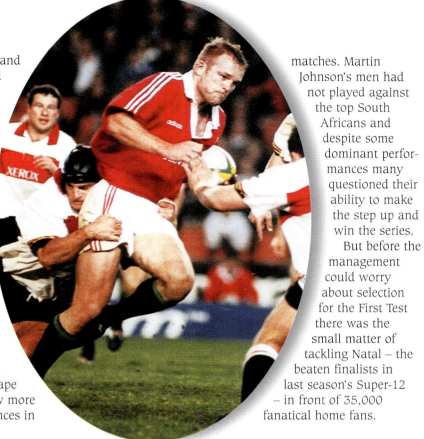

matches. Martin Johnson's men had not played against the top South Africans and despite some dominant performances many questioned their ability to make the step up and win the series.

But before the management could worry about selection for the First Test there was the small matter of tackling Natal – the beaten finalists in last season's Super-12 – in front of 35,000 fanatical home fans.

Natal 12
British Lions 42
June 14, Durban

Natal were no match for a rampant Lions side who produced their best rugby to date in a comprehensive 42-12 victory – a result which sent further shock waves through South African rugby.

Tries from Townsend, Catt and Dallaglio and another peerless kicking display from the

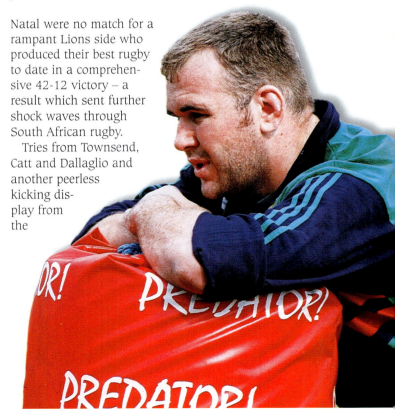

metronomic Jenkins – which yielded 24 points – were more than enough. There were also fine performances from Miller, who proved beyond doubt he could find the balance between attack and defence at the highest level, and Gibbs.

Collecting the ball in midfield, Gibbs broke two tackles and began to pick up speed when he was confronted by the massive frame of 19-stone Ollie Le Roux. Instead of trying to evade the prop, Gibbs dropped his shoulder and ran over him. South African rugby had never seen anything like it before. After the match Willie-John McBride, the captain of the victorious 1974 Lions who beat South Africa, paid tribute to the new Lions.

"They were outstanding, absolutely outstanding," McBride said. "I really believe they can now win the first Test which is always the most important one. Watching from afar on TV I had been encouraged by their inventiveness and running skills, but what I really wanted to see in the flesh against Natal was a commanding, physical and totally committed performance up front. The Lions delivered." However it was not all good news. After only 12 minutes they lost Robert Howley, who dislocated his shoulder falling awkwardly. The joy of the Natal victory was tempered with the realisation that they would have to complete the most demanding part of the tour without their inspirational Welsh scrum-half.

But in keeping with the spirit of the tour the Lions shrugged off their disappointment and flew south from Natal to Wellington in the mountainous Western Cape. One match to go against the Emerging Springboks side – and then the crunch. In the minds of the selectors the Test side was taking some shape and the final decision was going to make King Solomon's judgement look like a piece of simple arbitration.

Ian McGeechan summed it up: "We are going to have to leave out some players who are playing outstandingly well."

Emerging Springboks 22
British Lions 51
June 17, Wellington

The team selected to face the Emerging Springboks had the look of a second XV and featured late replacements Catt, Tony Diprose, who had replaced Quinnell, and Nigel Redman, Weir's replacement. Charged with securing a confidence-boosting win, the mid-week Lions were not found wanting and brushed aside the opposition 51-22, running in six tries to three. Northampton's Nick Beal was the star turn with a hat-trick of tries – the second of the tour – adding to scores from Stimpson, Catt and Rowntree, but attention was focused on other areas.

Back, knowing this was his last chance to push for a Test place, played a blinder – hunting down the opposition,

Beauty and the beast... Natal cheerleaders add a touch of glamour for the Lions visit, while (opposite), Tim Stimpson stands his ground against the Emerging Springboks

recycling the ball time and time again and acting as the crucial link between the pack and the Lions' supremely confident backs.

At full-back Stimpson showed he either hadn't been reading the papers or simply didn't care what they said. He produced a dazzling all-round display which belied the reports that Jenkins was a certainty for the No 15 shirt on Saturday.

The preparation was done and the might of the World Cup holders awaited the Lions in Cape Town. The Test team was announced on the Thursday before the game and, putting aside the joy or misery

of individuals, it looked the most balanced XV that could have been selected.

Veteran Evans, picked to play in his seventh consecutive Test after touring in both 1989 and 1993, caught the feeling of all the players as they contemplated the task ahead. "A lot of aches and pains have gone into this tour so far," Evans said. "At my age waking up in the morning after training is not a great experience, but selection makes it all worthwhile. In rugby terms you can not get better than the first Test of a Lions series against South Africa."

It was now almost time for the talking to stop...

FOUR

The First Test

WEDNESDAY morning, June 18th 1997 and somewhere inside an hotel nestling in the quiet of the hills on the outskirts of Cape Town a young woman is making her way down a corridor. In her hand she holds a pile of 35 letters. She comes to a door, bends down and pushes a letter under it. Another door, another letter, on and on she goes until the job is done.

For 15 men Samantha Peters was the bearer of very glad tidings – "selected for the first Test" – for another six it was disappointment tempered by a consolation "substitute" and for the remaining 14 it was "hard luck – but don't forget this is a three-match series".

The waiting was over – the jockeying for position done. The mission now was Lions for glory against South Africa. The destination the Newlands Stadium in Cape Town, the day of reckoning Saturday June 21st.

To reach this stage the Lions had battled for seven out of eight wins against provincial sides, starting somewhat slowly but improving by the game, showing glimpses of that total rugby philosophy which was deemed the key to success – forwards playing as backs, backs playing as forwards, quick ball, quick hands and decisive running.

The last outing before the Test selection meeting had been a 51-22 win over the Emerging Springboks. Fran Cotton, the tour manager, said that the Lions team would not be named until the Saturday of the Test. "It is something the South Africans did under Andre Markgraaff and we do not see any particular reason to help them by naming our team early," he said. It was a bluff.

Cotton and Ian McGeechan, the head coach, Jim Telfer the assistant coach and captain Martin Johnson locked themselves away for two hours of hard talking and near impossible choices. "It took longer to pick the team than it did the original squad," admitted Cotton later. The key debating points for McGeechan and company had been how to offset the loss of Robert Howley, should John Bentley play on the left wing, was Tim Stimpson the man for the full-back job and, the most keenly argued selection of them all, Richard Hill or Neil Back for the openside flank position?

The choice made, the letters dispatched – the idea being that everybody had time to reflect on their position before coming together – the Lions then went behind closed doors for training.

The men picked were: **Neil Jenkins, Ieuan Evans, Scott Gibbs, Jeremy Guscott, Alan Tait,**

[Facing] Steely eyed determination of the Lions' magnificent front row of Wallace, Wood and Smith. Jeremy Davidson [left] rises to the occasion in the line out.

Gregor Townsend, Matt Dawson, Tom Smith, Keith Wood, Paul Wallace, Martin Johnson, Jeremy Davidson, Lawrence Dallaglio, Richard Hill, Tim Rodber. The replacements: John Bentley, Mike Catt, Austin Healey, Barry Williams, Jason Leonard and Rob Wainwright.

In the party of 35 there were 21 Englishmen yet just six made the final line-up. The hopes rested on a Celtic blend and the small but mobile front three playing out of their skins. As Gregor Townsend said, the Lions were focused.

"People have seen our game plan and we are going to stick to it," he said. "The only qualification is that we must be patient. South Africa probably have the best defensive back-line in the world and we might have to go through nine or ten phases to break them down."

Saturday June 21, Newlands

South Africa 16
British Lions 25

Try heroes: Matt Dawson (right) goes over in the corner, while (facing page) Alan Tait and Neil Jenkins celebrate the Lions' second score. Boks' Gary Teichmann (below) was less impressed...

Known as "the home of South African rugby" the tight stadium with a 50,000 capacity was hosting a South Africa v Lions Test for the 12th time and the record book – already stacked against the Lions – delivered little comfort. The tourists had won there just three times.

Worse, for the English contingent, this was the scene of the 1995 World Cup debâcle where England had crashed out 45-29 to a rampant New Zealand side.

The wind was up, the crowd was baying and first blood went to South Africa. Edrich Lubbe kicked a penalty in the third minute but the lead was to last for just another four before the immaculate Jenkins brought the teams level. The home pack started to up the ante and the Lions front row was hanging on for dear life, never able to dominate at any stage.

In the 24th minute the home side scored a try which for many teams would have been a mortal blow. A lineout and an easy take for Mark Andrews. The ball went to Hannes Strydom and then to Os du Randt, the massive charging prop. The drive was too much for the visitors and South

Africa were ahead – the plot was going according to plan. Wallace, Smith and Wood, however, were not done. They steeled themselves for the fight, held solid in the scrums and even started to make dents in the South Africans in loose play. The back row was firing on all cylinders. Dallaglio, Hill and Rodber were causing problems round the fringes and getting in among the South African backs. The revelation, however, was Jeremy Davidson, whose lineout work was nothing short

of sensational.

On Lions' ball, up he went time and time again, the catch clean, his confidence soaring with each mighty take. Joost van der Westhuizen was always going to cause problems, but the Lions breakaway forwards were causing even him concern, and even more trouble for outside-half Henry Honiball. The pressure mounted and the South Africans, who were to suffer from indiscipline, gave the visitors a route back into the match. In the 34th minute Jenkins

stepped up to cut the lead to two points and then two minutes later he struck another perfect penalty. The Lions were ahead for the first time in the match and they held the lead to half-time, then extended it with another Jenkins penalty.

The tackling from the Lions was immense and nobody hit harder or did more damage than the amazing Gibbs. At 5ft 10in he is on the small side for international rugby – but Gibbs is about as wide as he is tall and

schooled in that hardest of places, rugby league. Smashing opponents into the ground is second nature to him and on top of that he had a cause for which, if necessary, he was going to lie down and die.

It is therefore astonishing to report that it was a Gibbs missed tackle which put South Africa back in the driving seat. Gary Teichmann, the Springbok captain, broke down the left, Gibbs powered in with the hit, but Teichmann just bounced out of it and fed Russell Bennett who went over. The home side led 13-12 after 43 minutes.

Bennett then seemed to score another try when Ruben Kruger and Andre Venter worked a clear passage down the left, but thankfully for the visitors the referee called them back for a forward pass.

Even so the lead grew to five points when Honiball landed a penalty in the 49th minute but Jenkins kicked a penalty in the 62nd minute and it was 16-15 to South Africa. The clock was running down, the moment of truth had arrived. The next

blow would almost certainly be decisive. A Lions back had not scored a try at Newlands since 1955 when Jeff Butterfield, the England and Northampton centre, crossed in a 25-9 defeat. At long last a Lions back was about to enter the same territory and what a score it was. By a strange twist of face it was to be another Northampton man who made it all possible,

The 72nd minute and the Lions had the put-in at a scrum about ten metres outside the South Africa 22. The ball came back, the Springbok backrow waited, anticipating another Rodber break. Instead Dawson picked up and broke down the blindside. Evans cut inside from the right and Dawson continued his arcing run chased hard by Teichmann, Venter and van der Westhuizen with Bennett backtracking and full-back Andre Joubert coming across to cover. Dawson, aware of Evans' run, and his own lack of space, lifted the ball into his right hand and made to lob the ball back inside. The hounds chasing stopped dead in their tracks, the scrum-half tucked the ball under his arm again and scuttled over for a tremendous individual score. Dawson grounded the ball and just kept on running. The 6,000 Lions supporters in Newlands erupted.

"I got a bit carried away with it all," he admitted later. "It was definitely a dummy and not an intended pass inside. I'm always looking for that sort of thing, but have not got away with it for a long time."

Jenkins missed the conversion and the Lions steeled themselves for the Springbok onslaught. It never happened. Instead the men in the red jerseys were back on the attack again as the clock ticked towards the final whistle.

Rodber and Dawson set up a run from a scrum, the ball was laid back and Townsend flipped it out for Gibbs who powered through the home midfield. Eventually halted, he made the ball available, Rodber gathered and sent Jenkins forward. He drew the defence and Tait arrived to score the try.

A remarkable result and a remarkable performance. The Lions were 1-0 up in the series, they had confounded just about everyone and their defence had been more than magnificent – it had been heroic. The looks of abject misery on the faces of the Springbok players said it all. Yet for all the glory, the rush and glow of victory, the Lions were remaining cool-headed. One win does not a series make.

"They will come back strong and, if we lose the next two, we will only have ourselves to blame," warned Johnson. "Whoever plays in the Second Test must work really hard because Test matches don't go to plan. You have to tackle and tackle.

"If we can do the business in Durban, then we'll celebrate because we have won the series. The South Africans will be baying for our blood and we will have to dig deeper if we are to win." But then pausing to enjoy the moment he added: "It is something you dream about, leading the Lions to victory in a Test in South Africa. Matt's try turned it for us, but Neil Jenkins kept us in there with his kicking."

For Dawson the match capped a remarkable return to the heights of international rugby. He played in England's 1996 Five Nations season but then in 1997 was dropped, finding himself behind Andy Gomarsall, Austin Healey

and Kyran Bracken in the pecking order. But for the injury to Howley who was a dead cert choice for the Test team prior to the tour, at best Dawson could only have aimed for a place on the bench.

Yet such was the incredible team-spirit created by this Lions party that foes of the Five Nations and rivals for Test spots formed an amazing and powerful bond. Dawson noted as much when he revealed how Howley, by this time back at home in Wales, had helped. "When Rob was here we worked together and I also did my homework studying videos of van der Westhuizen," said Dawson. "He then rang me from Wales and told me to stay in van der Westhuizen's pocket and to hound him all over the pitch. He also faxed me a good luck message." In one fell swoop Dawson had revived his international career – for not long after these heroics he was back in favour with England, summoned to play in a one-off Test against Australia in July scheduled just a little over a week after the Lions had returned home.

As for the Springboks the backlash was savage and recriminations within their dressing room unforgiving. "We made a lot of mistakes and handled below our best," said Carel du Plessis. "It was a disappointing display by our back line, but the Lions defence was solid and prepared to take on the opposition." There were no excuses from Teichmann who bought Dawson's dummy and virtually the shop to boot. "We thought he was going to pass," he said. For McGeechan, who like Cotton, had come out of that selection meeting days earlier admitting it was the toughest he had ever had, it was a glorious moment, a match that vindicated all of his coaching skills and his rugby philosophies.

"It's quite incredible," he said. "We knew we had a special bunch of players and they proved it. That was the toughest game we've ever been involved in and the Second Test will be massive for both teams.

"The defence was awesome and did us proud and we conceded one penalty for offside in a tight defensive situation which is a huge tribute to the organisation. The front row was compact and Jeremy Davidson had an excellent

display in the lineout. We are all in a different ball game as a squad because we have not won the first Test match of a series since 1974."

In fact everywhere you looked there were Lions performances to laud. Everyone had their own man of the match; from Gibbs, from Dawson, from Davidson, on and on went the list. What it proved was that all the players had done their bit, all had raised their game to a new level, and each and every man had played his socks off for the sake of the team and the whole party. If more evidence of that was wanted it came at the next training session where the whole squad turned out – even though those involved in the Test match had been given leave of absence. For Dr James Robson, there were the injuries to deal with; Townsend had X-rays for a knock in the ribs, prop Smith was recovering from a dead leg and Wood, the hooker, a twisted ankle. Eric Miller, the only player not available for selection for the Newlands game because of flu, was on the mend but now it was the turn of Simon Shaw to suffer from the same symptoms.

Those were the more immediate problems. The unforeseen one was a groin injury to Evans which was to rule him out of the rest of the tour so by the time of the next selection meeting the Lions management knew that they would have to make at least one change to the Test side.

The Second Test was to be played in Durban and the good point about the scheduling of the fixtures was that the Lions would not have to wait long to try to continue their winning run – a week between each of the three meetings never allowing the momentum to slack.

As for Cotton, McGeechan and Co it was back to selection, more debates, more cases to be made and more "Dear John" letters for Miss Peters to deliver ...

That champagne feeling (though a beer will do!). Lions stars Alan Tait, Matt Dawson and Neil Jenkins savour the moment, while Ieuan Evans shows the fans what victory means

Back on the Road

ONE up, two to go. Yet for the squad the euphoria of the First Test win in Cape Town had only been allowed to bubble on that famous Saturday night. All too soon it was back to work and minds on the next challenge. One step at a time. South Africa again loomed as the challenge at the end of the week, but first the Lions headed to Bloemfontein to face Free State – for the fourth and final match against a Super 12 provincial side.

Certainly no easy ride at the best of times especially as Free State could boast a proud record of never having conceded anything like 50 points against a touring side in 94 years. The team may have been missing five players on Springbok duty, but the fires of South African pride raged strong.

As for the Lions, there were men going on to the field that Tuesday afternoon – June 24th – determined to make the Lions Test team, to make a huge case for the selection meeting which would be held later that evening.

Captaining the Lions was Nigel Redman and he is worth a chapter of his own. The Bath second row stalwart had won 18 England caps between 1984 and 1994 – never in the team for any length of time and by 1997 his rugby thoughts were turning to coaching rather than playing. He arrived in South Africa having added one more England cap and with a cruel record of having been dropped ten times – even though there is nobody around who can remember him having a bad game. He tells the story of how

Jack Rowell the England coach broke the news about his elevation to Lions status. "I can't believe it," said Redman. "Neither can I," added Rowell.

"It gets better and better," he added – and indeed it did.

Free State 20
British Lions 52
Tuesday June 24, Bloemfontein

The score line only tells half a story – Free States' proud record of never conceding more than 50 points was gone. But there was much, much more to this match.

Will Greenwood, the only uncapped member of the Lions party, was knocked out in the game and out of the tour while Bentley scored a superb hat-trick.

Yet the real story was the Miller's tale. Eric Miller was magnificent. His aggression in attack, his ball handling and awareness, out of this world. In defence he was a giant, knocking them down left, right and centre and in Neil Back and Rob Wainwright the Leicester No 8 found two able and willing lieutenants.

Tim Stimpson and Jannie De Beer swapped penalties, but then the Lions hit their stride. Mike Catt kicked cross-field for Stimpson to score, Bentley then burst past two defenders for his first try and tore past another one for his second. Stephen Brink managed a try for Free State, but the Lions hit back.

Greenwood's scything midfield burst cleared the way for a simple score for Allan Bateman. Then came the Greenwood injury. Tackled and turned by Jaco Coetzee, Greenwood fell awkwardly, the back of his head hitting the hard South African ground with a mighty thump.

Wainwright, an Army doctor by profession, forgot the game to go to his colleague's assistance and an unconscious Greenwood was carried from the field. He soon came round, but

Bentley and Underwood (inset) leave the opposition grounded in the 52-20 victory over Free State

was kept in hospital overnight before being released, but out of the tour – concussion leading to a mandatory spell on the sidelines. On top of that he also damaged his shoulder

The selection meeting for the Second Test found Ian McGeechan, Jim Telfer, Fran Cotton and Martin Johnson with an easier job, but even so they were still prepared to discuss the team for long hours. They sat down knowing that they had got it right first time around and apart from the enforced change, Ieuan Evans out with a groin injury – Bentley in – that was to be the only tinkering done, although final selection was left to the Thursday evening.

Bentley, this time, ripped open his selection letter and later said, "It made so much better reading this week. When I was picked for the squad I set out to get a Test place and now I feel a real sense of achievement though with Ieuan's injury it was not in ideal circumstances."

A good win out of the way, the selection debate all but done, it was back to thinking about the next Test match and Durban. Telfer was well aware of the challenge to come: "South Africa will play through their forwards who probably had a few talkings-to. Remember South Africa had more of the game than us at Cape Town and good teams like the Springboks do not waste opportunities like that a second time. They will throw everything at us."

And as far as Johnson was concerned "everything" included the kitchen sink.

The Springboks, smarting from defeat, were forced into changes. Pieter Rossouw came in for James Small, Percy Montgomery, of Western Province, collected a first cap while Transvaal's Danie van Schalkwyk was recalled.

Andre Joubert, their full-back who was virtually anonymous in the First Test, was also threatening to up his performance levels. "I've been in this situation before and come out of it on top and I see no reason why that won't happen again," he said.

"When I went out at Newlands I didn't feel at ease, my confidence wasn't that high. My performance was below par and it was difficult for everyone coming together for the first time."

Indeed. It meant game on for Durban.

SIX

The Clincher

THERE was an air of tension in Durban from the moment the sun came up. This was a day of destiny, a startling moment of truth. The British Lions had confounded everyone by taking the First Test a week earlier and now they stood on the threshold of greatness.

The team, except for the unfortunate Ieuan Evans, was as it had been, and nobody was underestimating the size of the task ahead.

Even if the Lions lost there would be another chance to clinch the series but that thought never entered anyone's head. This was THE match – and it had to be won. Willie-John McBride's 1974 Lions had triumphed and worn the mantle of the greatest-ever Lions team with some dignity. Now it was the chance for the baby boomers to show that they too had grown up. It was going to be tough – but not in the wildest dreams of any of the players or the management had anyone realised just how tough.

To come through the hostile atmosphere, to survive the assault and to fulfil expectations that had gone from wanting little to wanting everything inside a week was going to be hard, but these Lions were bonded by an incredible sense of purpose and an absolute vision of the mission they had to complete. ➤

> 6 **South African rugby has a virile image; they like to breed massive, sturdy men and I guess someone like me knocking them over creates an identity crisis. I am sure they will be looking for me after last week**
> **– Scott Gibbs** 9

Traffic stopper ... the Lions fans on their way to the Second Test in Durban

Saturday June 28, King's Park, Durban

South Africa 15
British Lions 18

It was at King's Park in 1995 that South Africa came through the mud and rain storms to beat France 19-15 in the semi-finals of the World Cup. The rest, as we know, is history.

This time, however, there was no happy ending for the home side – they were beaten by a Lions team that tackled everything, every opponent, every opponent's shadow. Even so the Springboks scored three tries to none, then kicked the game away with a woeful performance from an array of penalty-takers. As for the Lions they found a likely hero playing an unlikely role.

Jeremy Guscott, the Bath and England centre, already had a place in Lions' folklore after an inspired try on the 1989 tour to Australia. One

The posts towered above him, but Guscott knew what to do. He dropped the ball, the leg was jacked back and the boot fired. He struck the ball cleanly and it sailed high and between the posts – the Lions had done it.

That was how the world ended for South Africa, but first, back to the beginning of the match. The atmosphere inside King's Park was electric – an intense feeling of expectation setting everyone on edge.

The players took the field, the Lions steely-eyed and determined, each and every man knowing this was it, a day of reckoning which would cement their places in the game's history. Then there were the Springboks – psyched up and snorting fury. They had everything to lose, they had taken a battering in the home press, they had been lambasted left, right and centre and yoked by a weight of expectation they were straining to snap.

The whistle went and the first exchanges were

awesome. As Jim Telfer had predicted South Africa were playing it through hard-driving forwards and the pressure on the Lions was colossal. Desperate, desperate defence was the order of the day, every man had to make his hit, make it big and make it count. The little guys had to bring down the South African giants and the big guys had to stoop down to take out the little 'uns. There were no hiding places.

The Springbok assault remained ferocious and threatening and the home side camped in the Lions half of the field for an incredible 80 per cent of the game and enjoyed 70 per cent possession. And they tried everything to unhinge the Lions. A week earlier Neil

down in the three match series, Guscott played in the second match with the Lions needing to win and wanting some magic to make it happen.

And he provided it. The ball came to him, Guscott, seeing the opposing back line was far forward, grub-kicked through the defence and ran on to collect his kick and score a try that saved the match and led to the Lions winning the series.

Fast forward eight years and to the three remaining minutes of the Second Test against South Africa. Here was Guscott, shamefully under-used by England in their 1997 Five Nations' campaign, collecting the ball from scrum-half Matt Dawson.

Jenkins had escaped, in the grand scheme of the match, relatively lightly. The number of high-balls dropped on him had been much lower than expected. Partly that was down to Andre Joubert, the brilliant South African full-back, having a surprisingly anonymous game and partly it was due to a tactical miscalculation.

This time it was snowing Gilbert rugby balls and Jenkins, a man caught between positions (is he a natural outside-half, is he a full-back?), was working overtime and proving himself a man of many talents. Some of those bombs he took clean, others escaped his grasp. When that happened, his team-

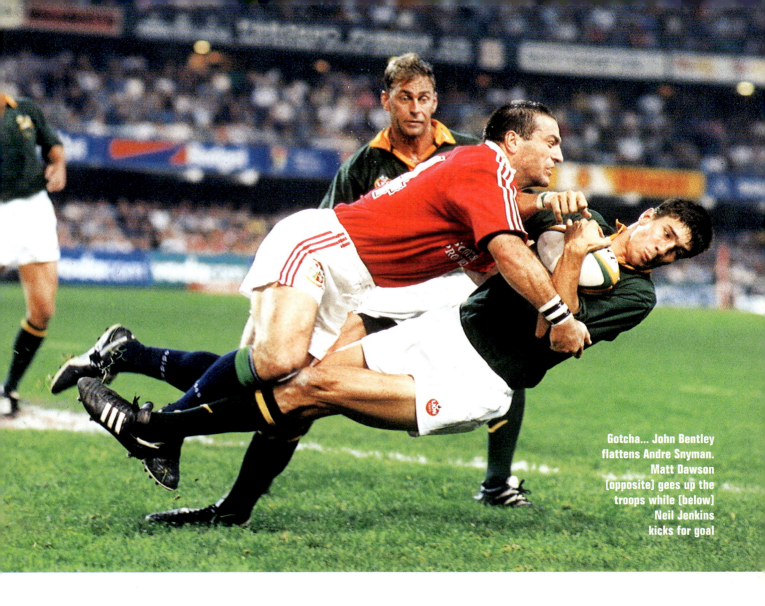

mates were quickly to the rescue. For almost half-an-hour the Lions rode the storm and amazingly took the lead when Jenkins stroked a long penalty between the posts. It was a short-lived joy because five minutes later South Africa scored their first try.

Another round of desperate defending found the Lions holding the line – but only just. Then the ball flipped up for Joost van der Westhuizen, the Springbok scrum-half acknowledged as the best in the position in the world. As Matt Dawson, his opposite number, had done a week earlier, van der Westhuizen decided to take them on himself and he squeezed over with a darting, low run.

The Springboks were ahead, but about to reveal their Achilles' heel. They could not kick a goal to save their lives and beating these Lions was infinitely more important than that. Henry Honiball at fly-half, new cap Percy Montgomery and Joubert had three conversion and three penalty attempts between them – and they fluffed the lot.

There could be no excuses. Conditions were ideal and Jenkins was making it all look so simple. Yet somehow the Springboks managed to scuff the most straightforward of kicks. This from a country where goal-kickers have been legend. What would Naas Botha make of it all? And how did Joel Stransky, the fly-half in the World Cup final and a spectator in the stand, feel as he witnessed their inept efforts? Still, van der Westhuizen's try put the home side ahead and gave them a scent of blood. But these Lions would not fold and, indeed, moments later took the lead again thanks to another fine penalty from Jenkins who was rubbing salt into a Springbok wound that was to become a fatal haemorrhage.

The Clincher

Against all the odds, against the run of play, the Lions reached half time leading 6-5. There seemed only two possible outcomes for the second half – the Lions would eventually crumble – or the Springboks would run out of steam. Neither was true. The finite time of the match was running down, urging players on both sides to push that bit harder, dig that bit deeper, the feeling persisting that whoever could strike first would rule. And initially it was woe for the Lions.

The second half was just a minute old when disaster struck. The Lions were immediately on the backfoot, but somehow had the ball and were trying to clear their lines. Alan Tait was wrapped up by the Springbok defence, but tried to free the ball with a reverse pass. He should have just held it tight and waited for reinforcements. Honiball seized it, played it out to Danie van Schalkwyk who moved it on to Montgomery and he had an unopposed run to the line.

"I thought that I had wrecked everything, dream over. Just a bloody nightmare," said Tait later.

That made it 10-6 to the home team, but Jenkins kept the Lions in touch with another penalty in the 46th minute. Yet still the Springboks came and still the defence was taking just about everything that was thrown at them.

Then in the 56th minute it seemed the Lions had blown it. Joubert had the ball in hand and facing him was John Bentley – a man who epito-mised the spirit and heart of the Lions and a man who had made some thrilling runs in the provincial games. Joubert went on the outside and a hand-off left Bentley clutching at thin air. He could only look up to read the name of Joubert's boot-maker as the Springbok full-back dived over in the corner. It was 15-9 to South Africa.

"I looked for a shovel so I could dig a hole and bury myself," said Bentley. "I felt shocking about making such a fool-ish mistake and I'd made it on the biggest stage in the world. I thought after that we were going to struggle."

Back came the Lions. Jenkins cut the gap to three points with 14 minutes to go, brought it all square with six minutes left and the Lions could scent control of their own destiny. Now, for once they were on the attack and Scott Gibbs, whose tackling had inspired his team-mates, set up a dazzling raid.

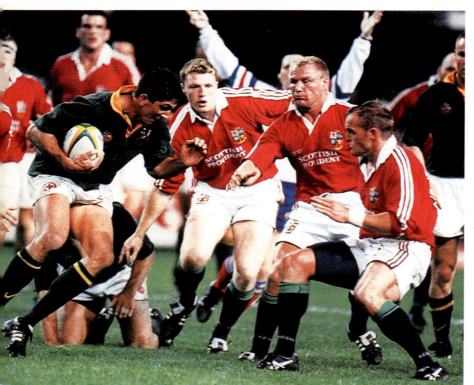

The Wales centre cut in on the South African defence from an angle, slicing it apart and there, standing in his way, was the gigantic Springbok prop Os du Randt, a full five stone heavier than the Swansea man. Most people would have gone for the side-step, the hip-swinging swerve, the team-mate in support. Not Gibbs. He just took du Randt on and flattened him – it was as if a mini had wiped out an articulated truck and come out of the collision in shiny show-room condition.

The defining moment was now close at hand. Keith Wood collected the ball and sent a deft grubber kick far up field forcing the Springboks to play it into touch – Lions throw in. The forwards lined up, shirts weighed down with blood and sweat, faces etched with deep lines of intense concentration and tiredness – one more big effort.

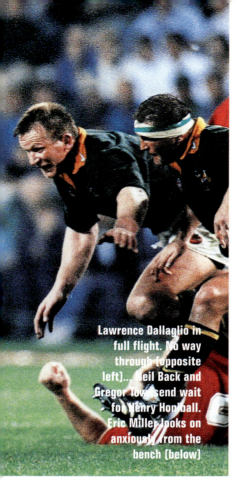

Lawrence Dallaglio in full flight. No way through (opposite left)... Neil Back and Gregor Townsend wait for Henry Honiball. Eric Miller looks on anxiously from the bench (below)

Wood took aim, up went Jeremy Davidson, his big safe hands gathering the ball. The Irishman had been magnificent a week earlier – he was even better this time and of the 14 clean takes in the lineouts that the Lions achieved, he was responsible for nine.

From Davidson the ball went to Dawson, and he was off round the tail of the line, with Gregor Townsend in support and the tireless backrow not far behind. Townsend went down near the line, the forwards piled in and Dawson had the ball. He looked out to his right and saw Guscott where he expected to see Townsend. "It was a planned move and we had called it," revealed Guscott. "Matt was looking for Gregor and when he wasn't there and he saw me, there was panic all over his face. The only thing on my mind was to go for the dropped goal." Guscott got it right and the Lions dug in for the final three minutes – more like five with injury time added on. The Springboks launched a last, desperate fling against a Lions side that now had substitutes on the field. Neil Back had come on for Richard Hill, Austin Healey for Tait and Miller for Rodber. Miller, so keen to get on the pitch, strained a muscle as he sprinted on.

There was time for Honiball to drop another bomb on Jenkins and he fumbled the collect, but Healey was quick to react and snuffed out the danger. A long kick and the ball went dead. Drop-out for the Lions from their 22. They checked with referee Didier Mene to find out if the whistle would go the next time the ball went dead. He confirmed it would, and safe in that knowledge, Jenkins hammered the ball out on the full. The whistle went and the Lions had done it – 2-0 up and unbeatable. The barmy army – the huge contingent of 5,000 British Isles supporters in the ground – went crazy and the Lions players joined in.

"There were a lot of errors, but unlike South Africa we took out chances and we actually played quite cleverly in the last 15 minutes," said McGeechan prior to fulfilling his side of a bet that if the Lions won he would let Keith Wood shave his head.

"But the show does not stop here, winning the Third Test is important, especially as we will look to eradicate the mistakes we made," he added.

Martin Johnson, never the most emotionally demonstrative of people, said: "This was the best day of my rugby life. Everyone, players and management, can be very proud of themselves."

Fran Cotton, the Lions manager, summed it up when he said: "Nothing can beat this moment – sheer character dug us out and I'm absolutely delighted."

For the Lions it was a night to enjoy, for the Springboks a night of misery to be followed by the inevitable headlines the next day ➤

– "BLUNDER BOKS BLOW SERIES" and "IT'S HEARTBREAKING". Carel du Plessis, the Springbok coach knew they were coming. "We have lost a Test series and that is unacceptable," he said. "All credit must go to the Lions, they just stuck in there."

Gary Teichmann, the South Africa skipper, added: "You've got to take your chances in any Test match and we were guilty of missing a number of opportunities to score. It's hard to believe that we lost but a game lasts for 80 minutes and in the end we were struggling to keep the Lions out."

And Teichmann was right. Based on terms of possession and territory the Lions had pulled off the crime of the century, the biggest steal of modern sporting times. Conceding three tries, scoring none, it could not have been weighted any more heavily against them. But South Africa, because of their inept kicking, let victory slip through their fingers and the iron will of the Lions team to succeed proved irresistible. By not scoring those goals, it was as if they were saying to the Lions: "There's the prize – you take it if your dare." They did.

Later the Lions prepared to move on for Vanderbijlpark, 50 kilometres south of

Johannesburg and as they boarded their coach the entire hotel appeared to send them on their way with a rendition of the Shosholoza song – the theme which was the anthem for the Springboks in the 1995 World Cup.

These Lions – all 35 of them – had become rugby legends and had been heroes in a drama of compelling intensity which thankfully had the right ending. British sport and the feelgood factor don't often go hand in hand – but on July 29th 1997 they did – in fact it was more than feelgood, it was a feel-bloody-great factor.

Jeremy Guscott pulls the trigger to clinch the series in thrilling fashion – and the celebrations begin! First with the attention of Scott Gibbs and Neil Jenkins (inset). At the end, John Bentley leads the chorus as the Lions fans start a long, noisy evening of unbridled joy

Every Man A Hero

Welsh wizard ... the metronomic accuracy of Neil Jenkins' boot and the bulldozer tackles of Scott Gibbs broke the hearts of the Springboks

EVERY hour has its hero and the Lions tour of South Africa was one of many hours and many heroes. Every player in the party rose to the challenge and to a man played to a peak, lifting standards above what they were accustomed to at either club or Five Nations level. To succeed they needed to excel and they did without exception.

To single out individuals from such a collective effort is as difficult as it is unfair and there can be no debate that the tour threw up a plethora of stars, modest to a man.

Of the established internationals Neil Jenkins, Scott Gibbs, Jeremy Guscott and Tim Rodber immediately spring to mind. All four, respected and feared in their own right, found that little extra when it mattered most.

Jenkins was phenomenal. Without the Pontypridd points-machine the Lions would have lost the Test series and there can be no greater tribute than that. His kicking was truly awe-inspiring in its metronomic accuracy. Every time he stepped up to take a shot at goal, whether it was in the fraught atmosphere of the Tests or the more uninhibited surroundings of a midweek fixture, you felt he could not miss. Time and time again he did it, converting Lions' pressure into points and his five-from-five penalties in the second Test in Durban paved the way for Guscott's headline-grabbing 76th minute drop goal.

"It's a huge day. I've been on the end of a few hidings from the Springboks playing for Wales and that makes this

achievement even more satisfying," he said. "They scored three good tries and missed all their kicks whereas I was lucky enough to kick all of mine. We were quite lucky really. The main thing going through my mind when I'm kicking is that I'm back on the training field, block out the crowd and get the points required."

South African rugby is notorious for its willingness to kill the ball when the opposition threaten, but the presence of Jenkins made them think twice about infringing anywhere within their own half which, in turn, allowed the Lions to pursue their open, expansive game plan.

His fellow countryman Scott Gibbs had no less of an impact and became a talisman for the tour as the man capable of taking the Springboks on physically and winning. When Gibbs broke with the ball midway through the second half of the Durban Test and humbled the mighty Os du Randt with an even more mighty shoulder-charge, putting the 20 stone prop on his backside, he dented more than du Randt's ego. The Free State man is, or perhaps was, a cult figure in South Africa – gigantic, powerful and utterly unyielding. That he was flattened by Gibbs was a massive psychological blow.

The Swansea powerhouse was equally influential throughout the rest of the tour and was central to the pattern of play. Time after time the ball was moved to Gibbs who bulldozed his way up the middle where he set up quick ball for the rest of the team to start the attack again.

And with the added security of a man he described as 'the fastest prop in world rugby' next to him, Jeremy Guscott also flourished, making a mockery of Jack Rowell's decision to omit him from England's 1997 Five Nations campaign. It was clear from early on that the South Africans genuinely feared Guscott's ability to conjure something from nothing. Twice

he scored two tries in a match – against Eastern Province XV and Northern Transvaal.

A veteran of three Lions tours, Guscott produced some of the best form of a distinguished career. His defensive work – all too often overlooked – was relentless and whenever the Springboks charged at the Lions' midfield the Bath man was there to snuff out the danger.

Guscott's match-winning drop-goal in the Second Test, courtesy of one of the laziest swings of the boot you are ever likely to witness on the international scene, was merely the icing on the cake for the man who showed why he is dubbed 'The Prince of Centres'.

After the game, Guscott said: "The ball appeared at the base of a ruck and Dawson picked it up and looked around for Townsend – he saw me and had panic written all over his face. You look up at the posts and a little doubt does creep into you mind. You think 'What will they say if I miss it?' but then you tell yourself 'I've got to do it. It's got to go over'.

"I took the ball, kicked it and prayed. It floated over the posts and I heard this enormous roar. It was unbelievable. It seemed like ages until the final whistle, but when I heard it I looked up into the crowd to see my mum. I didn't see her, but I knew she wouldn't have to buy a drink that night."

Up front much depended on Tim Rodber, both in terms of experience and the way he tackled the fearsome South African forwards. Rodber, the Northampton skipper, had been superb on England's

1994 tour to South Africa and again he rose to the challenge. He was the rock around which the Lions first two Test victories were built. A relatively small, mobile front row for the Tests meant the Lions pack needed an 'enforcer' – the big man capable of putting in the shuddering hit – and Rodber was that man. Whenever the South Africans sent one of their forwards charging towards the gain line, there was Rodber to dip his shoulder and send them back from whence they came.

The big names did the business, but it was the previous unknowns who gave the Springboks the biggest shock. The squad, bar Leicester's Will Greenwood, had full international honours but many had only a handful of caps won in the Five Nations – a tournament light years away from the intense demands of South Africa. That daunted no-one.

The two props, Paul Wallace and Tom Smith (three Scotland caps), epitomised this dogged determination. There is no harder place than the dark world of the front row, but both men excelled. Early on in the tour the Lions scrum creaked under the pressure applied by the provincial sides and the Springbok front row must have been licking their lips in anticipation of tearing the Lions to shreds in the Tests.

Yet within a month Wallace and Smith, with a little help from that wily old campaigner Jim Telfer, had cemented the apparent weakness and the anticipated slaughter of the British scrummage never happened. Their dynamic loose play, cover tackling and ball-handling gave the Lions' play a vital extra dimension and there can few higher compliments in the British game than to be selected ahead of Jason Leonard. Behind Wallace and Smith in the Test

scrum there was a young Irishman who began the tour as a promising forward and came home a fully-fledged star. Jeremy Davidson was a revelation.

When the final Lions squad was announced it seemed certain the colossal Simon Shaw would partner Johnson in the second row, but somebody forgot to tell Davidson. From his very first appearance, as a substitute for Doddie Weir against Eastern Province, the London Irish man was irrepressible. As the tour wore on his case for inclusion in the Test side became undeniable.

In the Tests Davidson was up against Mark Andrews – acknowledged as one of the best second row forwards in the world – but the tenacious 22-year-old did not flinch. Such was his dominance in the line-

out that Johnson repeatedly called the Lions throw to his No 4 rather than himself.

Another Irishman who started the tour as a promising young player and returned a hero was Leicester's Eric Miller, who forced Tim Rodber to dig deep to hold on to his Test place. A very different type of player from his Northampton rival, Miller embodied the fast-moving, quick-thinking approach that Fran Cotton and Ian McGeechan worked so hard to instil.

What a season it had been for the No 8. He displaced Dean Richards from the Leicester first team and made his full international debut. Now he was with the Lions. Miller seemed to be everywhere in the games he played. His tireless running with and without the ball breathed life into countless attacks and his defensive work was top notch.

The perfect foil for Miller was his dynamic club team-mate Neil Back who had the ideal chance to silence his knockers who claimed he

Crowning moment of a memorable tour for Jeremy Guscott

was too small for international rugby. Discarded by England on the basis of a few inconclusive performances, Back was clearly out to make a point. Everybody knew about his punishing support play and ability to link between the backs and forwards, but few suspected he was capable of some of the shuddering tackles he put in on South Africa's big men.

And so to the backs where there were men who eclipsed anything they had achieved before. The loss of scrum-half Robert Howley was a huge blow but Matt Dawson, his replacement, was a sensation. His sublime solo try which dragged the Lions into the first Test in Cape Town will be his best-remembered contribution, but it was in so many other areas that he produced the goods when they were needed.

Lining up against Joost van der Westhuizen did not faze the Northampton man and he was ice-cool even when the temperature was reaching critical point around him. One of the most enduring memories of the First Test – and the tour as a whole – was the sight of du Randt thundering towards the Lions defence only to be unceremoniously upended by Dawson, some five stone lighter. Dawson also scored a magical try in the Third Test in Johannesburg, his two delightful Phil Bennett-esque side-steps taking him past the flailing tacklers for the Lions' only five-point score of the afternoon.

However, the indisputable star-turn was John Bentley – Bentos to his friends – who showed why Cotton had turned to the former rugby league man instead of some of the more established names in British rugby union. The Yorkshireman was electric and it was fitting that he should finish the tour as the joint leading try-scorer with seven.

Bentley scored the try of the tour with a 70-yard dash to sink the Gauteng Lions and his brace against Western Province were no more than his unstinting efforts deserved. Disappointed by not being selected for the First Test, Bentley responded in the only way he knew how – on the pitch. His hat-trick against Free State was typical of

the fiercely competitive nature of the man and would surely have secured him a Test spot even if Ieuan Evans had not been forced out with a groin injury. Bentley loved the physical and confrontational atmosphere and always looked to counterattack.

But if you want a hero who embodied the spirit of the 1997 Lions look no further than Rob Wainwright. From day one the Scotland skipper was the heart and soul of the Lions effort. He cajoled, encouraged and inspired all those around him with an infectious desire to win. Even though Lawrence Dallaglio was clearly pencilled in for the blindside spot in the Tests, Wainwright did not waver. But that is not to say he was merely a good tourist, making up the numbers and letting the 'true' stars get on with the job. Wainwright was as dynamic and influential as any of his colleagues.

A nine-minute hat-trick, a British Lions record, against Mpumalanga was as devastating a contribution as any and he was passionately committed to the success of the tour. He scored a crucial try in the narrow 18-14 victory over Border in East London and led by example with his tireless support work both on and off the field. He got his just reward – a Lions cap in the Third Test in Johannesburg, when Dallaglio switched to No 8 in place of Rodber. Although the battered and bruised Lions team lost, it would probably have been by much more if not for Wainwright's heroic defence.

Action men... Neil Back slips a despairing tackle (opposite), while Jeremy Davidson, who rose above everybody's expectation, wins another priceless line-out ball

Broken **Dreams**

FEW of us realise our dreams, climb to that pinnacle and survey the world from the very top – but for the party of 35 players selected to go to South Africa for the 1997 Lions tour the dream was within reach, a magnificent reality from the moment they stepped on to the plane.

To win everything was the aim of the party – but most important was beating the Springboks in the Test series. For the players, as individuals, the ultimate would be playing in that Test series. And of that party of 35 only 15 could be on the pitch at the same time. Disappointment was inevitable, but there was mighty consolation to be had by being in the party.

Yet the history of Lions tours and the nature of rugby is such that injury will always play a part. Every tour has its casualties and heart breaks. It is inevitable that some players will come home early, the chance for Lions glory – they tour only once every four years – gone forever. Genuine sympathy goes

to those who fail to last the distance but as they say, life goes on.

When a player is lost to the tour, a door opens for another man – and the extras drafted in during the Lions trip of 97 certainly found themselves enjoying a sweet summer that many of them could never have expected.

The Lions of 97 were not long into their programme before they lost their first man – Paul Grayson, the Northampton and England outside-half. Grayson had been suffering with a hip-muscle injury picked up in early March by which time he was selected for the tour. Wild horses were not going to stop him from doing everything humanly possible to be there. Grayson worked and worked to be fit, sat out the first match of the tour, but started against Border, a hard fought 18-14 win for the Lions. It was clear he still had problems and two days later he was gone from the tour.

"Disappointment doesn't come bigger than this and now I'll have to wait four years

A rare moment of relaxation on the beach for team doctor James Robson, one of the busiest men on tour as the hard grounds and even harder opponents took their toll of the Lions, like Keith Wood (inset)

for the next Lions tour," said Grayson as he packed up. "I felt it go in training, but still felt I could get through although it was sore and hampered my game – not that I am using it as an excuse."

Room for sentiment is tight at the best of times in sport, but Fran Cotton, the Lions manager, could understand Grayson's position. "People desperately want to play for the Lions and sometimes emotion takes over the clear thought process," he said. "We have all done that from time to time, but a decision had to be made and we need 35 fit men to select from to complete a tough schedule."

Mike Catt, in Argentina with England, received the summons. He had always been in the frame for selection in the first place and to many his omission was a surprise. Now he was on board and on the road to the ultimate honour – a Test place. Not that England, who had just produced a handsome 46-20 win over Argentina, were seeing it that way. They felt they had been rail-roaded into releasing the player.

According to Jack Rowell, the England coach, he claimed he was told that if Catt was not released, Arwel Thomas would be summoned by the Lions and his man would have missed the opportunity of a lifetime. Such moral pressure, if it was exerted, would have left Rowell with no option.

"It's a great opportunity for me, not necessarily to prove a point to anyone, but to enjoy the rugby," said Catt, South African-born but hitched to England colours. "Hopefully I can take this chance with both hands."

A week later and the casualty list was growing. A second man was coming home. Doddie Weir, the Scotland lock, was perhaps the unluckiest of all the potential Test Lions because he was kicked out of the tour following an unprovoked attack in a convincing win over Mpumalanga. Rob Wainwright had scored a first-half

hat-trick of tries and the Lions were on their way to a 64-14 triumph. But then, in the 57th minute, Weir's world came apart. A ruck formed and from behind Mpumalanga lines came the boot of one Marius Bosman. It made contact with Weir's knee and that was it for the Scot. He was taken for a scan to see whether he had damage to the cruciate as well as the medial ligaments of his left knee. Either way it was serious. Cotton was

Graham Rowntree (far left) was patched up, but for Doddie Weir (main picture and inset) a serious knee injury spelled the end of his tour

fuming: "My priority is to ensure that the Lions are properly protected by the referee," he said. "It's a hard enough game as it is without gratuitous violence, which tragically from Doddie's point of view has ended his tour."

Bosman was subsequently fined £1,500 which, Cotton drily noted, "would not cover Doddie's consultant's fees". Weir, once patched up, returned to South Africa to watch the third and final Test of a tour in which he had played four solid matches.

And so once again Rowell found his England squad being plundered. This time for Nigel Redman. The Bath lock, capped 19 times by England, had only made the England trip after Martin Bayfield pulled out. Now he was being asked to accept the game's ultimate honour.

Redman called his selection "unbelievable" and indeed only a few weeks earlier it had been

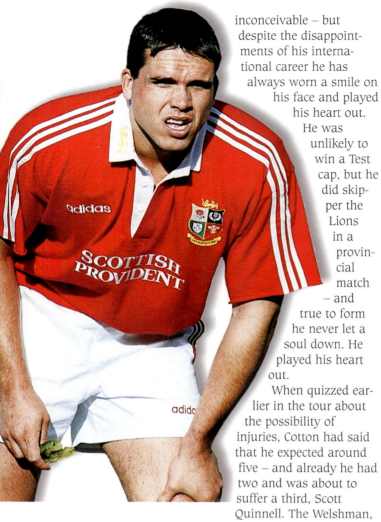

inconceivable – but despite the disappointments of his international career he has always worn a smile on his face and played his heart out. He was unlikely to win a Test cap, but he did skipper the Lions in a provincial match – and true to form he never let a soul down. He played his heart out.

When quizzed earlier in the tour about the possibility of injuries, Cotton had said that he expected around five – and already he had two and was about to suffer a third, Scott Quinnell. The Welshman, one of the prodigals back from rugby league, had suffered with a groin problem at the start of the 1996-97 season, but it had appeared to clear up.

A storming season with Richmond, followed by a brilliant try for Wales against Scotland, marked him out as a man back to form – better than before because rugby league with Wigan had toughened him up. The No 8 was sad but philosophical about the injury which suddenly flared up again in a 35-30 defeat by Northern Transvaal in Pretoria.

"The groin is inflamed and it looks like I'll need need six to eight weeks rest to get it right," he said.

The subsequent re-jigging of the squad meant that Eric Miller could contest his natural position of No 8 while the widely expected call for Ben Clarke, of England, to come to the rescue did not materialise. Instead the SOS went to Tony Diprose, the 25-year-old Saracens skipper. Much respected but untried at international

level – he won his first two England caps in Argentina – the player was as astounded as everyone to receive the summons.

There is no doubt that the backrow was one of the Lions' strengths. Neil Back, Lawrence Dallaglio, Tim Rodber and Richard Hill were and are world class. Rob Wainwright is a handy player and Diprose had little prospect of Test honours.

Even so he was a willing work-horse and proved in the few matches he played that his reputation is well-deserved, his ball-handling skills and awareness, particularly, were top drawer.

It never rains, as they say, but it pours, Three blows suffered and the fourth was not long coming. At the time it seemed catastrophic and it is not difficult to see why, although it is satisfying to look back and find the doom-laden scenario it raised not substantiated. Remember, this 1997 party was written off before it stepped on the plane and the only hope it seemed rested with one player – Robert Howley of Wales and Cardiff.

Howley was rightly seen as the key man among the key men. A brilliant scrum-half and the one player who was a Test certainty before the tour began. He had burst upon the international scene for Wales in 1996, scored a try in his first game against England and gone on to win 16 caps. Fast, strong – he was and is the complete scrum-half.

Howley was going to be up against Joost van der Westhuizen, acknowledged as the best scrum-half in the world. The Lions were in desperate need of him to nullify van der Westhuizen and bring some spark to their play.

As for the best-laid plans, they came apart 12 minutes into the game against Natal on June 14th. Howley dislocated his shoulder and

Tony Diprose is a picture of determination (opposite left), veteran Nigel Redman prepares for battle (below, opposite). Anxious moments... Lions players and staff look worried after Will Greenwood falls heavily against Free State. Flying Scotsman... late replacement Tony Stanger (below) in his one game for the Lions, against Free State

was eventually helped from the field. Matt Dawson replaced him and the wounded Lions put in a fighting performance to take the game 42-12. It was quite clear, however, that Howley would play no further part in the tour. An operation and four months of rest beckoned.

Like Grayson, Howley had hoped he could play his way through the pain and tried to stay on the pitch, lasting eight more minutes after the original knock. "I thought it was serious when it happened, but hoped against hope that maybe there was a chance I could just play my way through it, but as soon as I tried to throw a pass off my left hand it was very painful and I knew I was in big trouble."

Later, and accepting the blow as philosophically as he could, Howley added: "It could be much worse. We're not talking about a life threatening thing.

I've still got two arms and two legs.

"That said it is the biggest disappointment of my career and the biggest setback I ever expect to have. There were lots of tears when I phoned home and it still hasn't sunk in. I've devoted so much time and effort to the Lions and suddenly I'm on the plane back home."

But Howley, as shrewd as he is nifty on the field, got it right when he added: "We are still going to win the series 2-1."

Cotton had to be upbeat: "This disappointment will not deflect us from the task. It was a total accident, one of those injuries that happen in a game of rugby."

To fill the gap the Lions selected their third England scrum-half when they sent for Kyran Bracken, and it meant that he joined Dawson and Austin Healey in the battle for a Test spot, the three of them having been involved in an in-and-out struggle for an England place over the last two seasons. Dawson was to get the nod, in

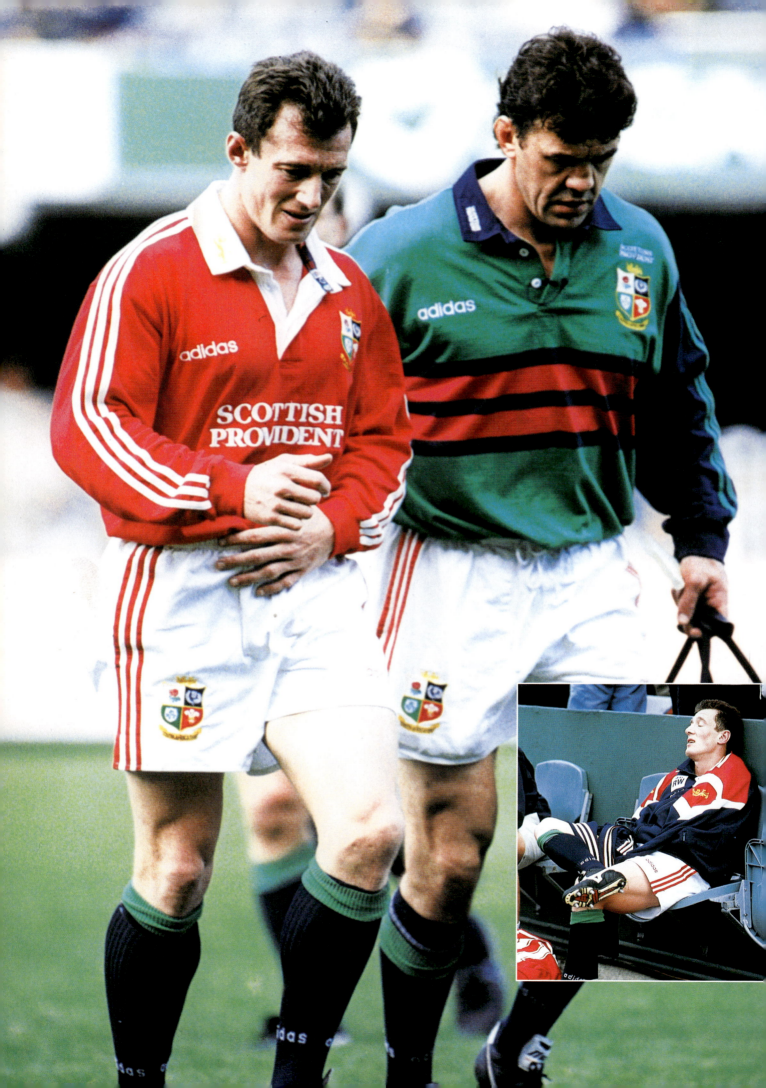

fact Dawson was to be a revelation. He was always good – but was he really THAT good? His performance in the First Test, won 25-16, was quite outstanding and if he did not quite produce the same spectacle in the other two matches, then he was still there threatening mayhem in the Springbok ranks.

And in fact Howley, though gone, was still an influence on the party having built a good rapport with Dawson. Howley phoned Dawson before the First Test to talk about van der Westhuizen and discuss the game. Then, on the morning of the Cape Town match Dawson received a good luck fax from Howley.

When the game was done, the battle was won, Howley was one of the first people on Dawson's "must ring" list. "I have the greatest respect for Rob and the way he was playing on tour, he was desperately unlucky, but he would want me to make the most of my opportunity which will involve a monumental effort. Rob deserved to be No 1 for the Test position and realistically my aim was to be on the bench."

The fifth casualty was the grand old man of the tour – Ieuan Evans. At 33 some may have thought he was past it as a winger at this level, but Evans is the complete footballer and his form on the tour had been outstanding. On top of that, he brought huge experience to the squad – he was on the Lions tour of 1989 when they won the series in Australia 2-1 and his try in the decider virtually settled the issue. He won three more Lions caps in New Zealand in 1993 and was again a key man.

Evans has had his knocks down the years – five dislocated shoulders, a broken leg and a dislocated ankle – but this time it was a groin injury which ended it for him. The dislocation was suffered by Will Greenwood, flattened in a tackle during the 52-30 win over Free State.

Greenwood, the only uncapped player in the original squad, hit his head with a fearful bang and was concussed. Worse, he had a dislocation of the shoulder which would keep him out of action for two months.

The Lions were fortunate that the competition for places in the backs was so fierce. John Bentley, as deserving as any, picked up Evans' wing place while, for the Third Test, Tony Underwood came in for Alan Tait. Tony Stanger, on tour in South Africa with Scotland, was called up and played one game – the 67-39 win over Northern Free State. Of the original squad, Peter

Clohessy, playing for Queensland, was the only non-starter, withdrawing from the squad because of an injured back, and that opened the door for the Saracens and Ireland prop Paul Wallace. Like his brother Richard, who was on the trip four years earlier as a replacement for Ian Hunter, Wallace was one to make the most of his chance and this sense of déjà vu. "It must be a family trait," observed Wallace when he was told to bring his passport.

So Catt and Wallace of the outsiders made it to win Test caps, while the others played their part. The likes of Diprose can come again in four years, Redman can look back on a rich experience that he never expected, Kyran Bracken moved back into the frame in the private war for the England scrum-half berth while Stanger picked up a prized red jersey from his detour.

Howley, because he deserved it so much, might come again while the rest of the disappointed, Grayson, Weir and Quinnell will find themselves battling with a new generation of players come 2001. The fact is that injuries were inevitable – it is the way the Lions coped with them which is so laudable. Everyone who appeared on the pitch at any time during the 13-match tour will be entitled to say they were in the Lions tour of 97. They can be proud of that, as they can be proud of the example they set and the bonds they forged.

"We picked players we knew could fit into the style of rugby we felt we had to adopt to beat the World Cup holders," said Cotton. "That led to a few selections not everyone agreed with, but there hasn't been one, not a single player, who hasn't come up to scratch out here."

Enough said. This tour, through the tears of joy and tears of sorrow, was an unqualified success in which every man was a key player in his own way.

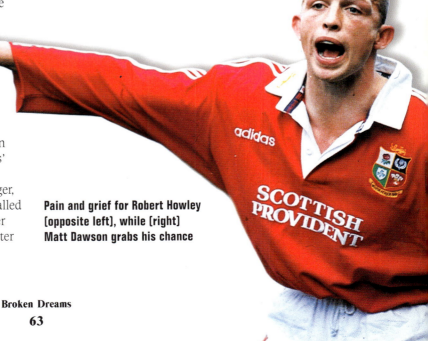

Pain and grief for Robert Howley (opposite left), while (right) Matt Dawson grabs his chance

CENSUS · 5 MILLION
S. AFRICANS MISSING
PRESUMED EATEN BY LIONS!

Lions' fans in party mood while (far right) John Bentley takes on Joost van der Westhuizen

N I N E

The Third Test

MISSION accomplished and a week to go – the Lions could afford to lie back and bask in the sun and their glory knowing that whatever happened in the next seven days they could go home, heads held high, pride intact, the British public looking forward to cheering their heroes.

That is how it might have been but this first professional tour was just that, professional. In the short time that rugby has been like that the players have grasped the responsibilities that come with a pay packet remarkably quickly and with such authority that they have made some other areas of the game's administration look an amateur shambles.

That much, however, could not be said of the Lions organisation. From head to toe and back again it had been meticulous and the homework and hard work had been rewarded handsomely.

Days later and in the afterglow of the Durban triumph, the sun beat down on Vanderbijlpark. The Lions were holed up in an hotel where there were few distractions. The management had planned it that way. As Fran Cotton admitted: "We anticipated the series being 1-1 at that stage and the hotel was chosen with that in mind. If anything it worked out that it was more suitable than we could have imagined. The

last week on tour is very difficult but we had an opportunity to recharge our batteries though the players were determined that the total focus would be on maintaining our form for the last two games. Mental preparation was the key to the week."

For a number of the party the game against Northern Free State at Welkom was going to be the last opportunity for wearing the famous red Lions jersey – and for two of the squad, the first and last. Kyran Bracken had flown in two weeks earlier having abandoned his holiday in Tobago to answer the call while the Scotland winger, Tony Stanger, was a late arrival for the injured Will Greenwood. A lifetime of sporting dreams are made by such moments. It was off to Welkom and those two were ready to make their first appearances for the Lions.

Northern Free State 39
British Lions 67
Tuesday July 1, Welkom

And so it came to pass that the Lions midweek expeditions into the heartlands of South African rugby passed as an unqualified success – six matches played, six matches won. This final outing also produced the highest score of the tour, the most points scored against the tourists and a rough edge of controversy.

Both Cotton and coach Ian McGeechan felt that the home side – known as the Purple People Eaters because of their lurid strip – had been a little too free with the boot.

"There were two or three stamping incidents which I find totally unacceptable," roared Cotton later. "The pitch was bone hard and the discipline of their players and the referee was not up to the standard we expect. We will be looking at the video and will be taking the appropriate action, ie citing, if the evidence is clear."

McGeechan too, was in voluble form: "It could have been dangerous out there. We've tried to play the game in the right way over here – you can't play the style of rugby we've aspired to without immense self-discipline and most of our opponents have showed discipline too."

The locals, particularly coach Pote Human, were rather bemused, but within 48 hours the anger had rather subsided with Cotton saying that there would be no official complaints, although certain points would be made to Northern Free State.

And so to the match. It took just 76 seconds for the Lions to score their first of ten tries when Tony Underwood, who was to go on and complete a hat-trick in the opening 23 minutes, went over. And an on-song Tim Stimpson was to keep the scoreboard ticking along nicely as the first half became a try-feast which promised, at one stage, to give the Lions a three-figure score.

By half-time they were 43-12 ahead and the opposition had a rather dubious penalty try to thank for five of those points.

Once in the clear by such a wide margin, the Lions eased off the gas and the defence became a little slack allowing the home team to score a total of five tries. Underwood's first half salvo was followed by two tries for Simon Shaw, two for Stimpson and one each for Bracken, Mark Regan and Neil Back.

The downside – an injury to Bracken which led to him being replaced by Austin Healey and Jason Leonard, captain for the day, replaced by Graham Rowntree. It was not a bad ending to the midweek matches but, curiously, the 39 points conceded were the most a Lions team had ever allowed to be scored against them and, despite playing some exciting open rugby, the Lions had their enthusiasm dulled by the fact that Northern Free State were meant to be the worst side of the tour.

The real problems with regard to the Third Test in Johannesburg were the injuries. Leonard had a torn thigh muscle, Alan Tait and Keith Wood groin strains and Eric Miller a strained thigh. It would make the last selection – the team to hopefully do a whitewash on South Africa – some job and raise interesting questions. Would this most professional of organisations turn sentimental and reward the likes of Neil Back with a Lions start?

Rob Wainwright (left) on the charge while (above) Matt Dawson reaches out for a try in the Third Test. The front rows (far right) engage in combat

SATURDAY July 5 – Ellis Park, Johannesburg

South Africa 35
British Lions 16

Hindsight reveals that this was a match too far, yet for most of it the Lions were playing some of their best rugby of the tour and indeed, deep into the second half it could as easily have swung their way as it did the Springboks.

What it comes down to, however, is raw, desperate hunger. The Lions had won the series and however magnificently they stirred themselves it was always going to be a job to match a Springbok team driven to the point of fury by their lack of success.

The Lions made three changes because of injury. Underwood for Tait, Mike Catt for Gregor Townsend and Regan for Wood. The switch was Neil Back for Richard Hill in the backrow and the Leicester man was delighted.

"I thought the chance had passed me by and it's going to be the pinnacle of my career and a huge opportunity." This was the sort of sentimental decision that carried no weight of risk.

Indeed, throughout the tour places had been contested by a squad who had given their all and as McGeechan said there were many deserving cases who went unrewarded. "There are players in this tour party who will not be playing in a Test even though they would have made the side on merit on other tours," he said. Catt's arrival and subsequent place in the team marked a transformation as remarkable as that of Matt Dawson. One day England reject – next, top of the world. The task they faced in the hot-house atmosphere of Ellis Park was going to be enormous. Here was a crowd of 61,000 and there were the Lions attempting to become the first side to whitewash the Springboks – not even Willie-John McBride's magnificent all-conquering side of 1974 had managed that, they drew the final

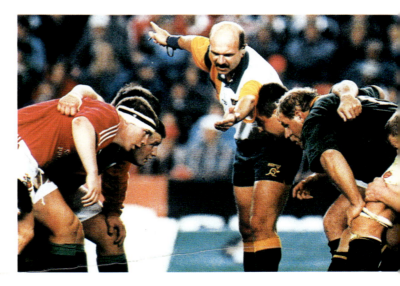

Test. The All Blacks, too, had not managed it and the last "to nil" series defeat was pre-20th century.

"It would be a lie if I said it wasn't going to be difficult," said Lawrence Dallaglio without the vaguest hint of a sigh or understatement.

In fact the Lions backrow was to change again with Tim Rodber forced to make way for Rob Wainwright because of a stomach muscle injury. And as before the Springboks came charging out of the blocks but the first real chance came with a Lions counter attack, Jeremy Guscott haring down the left wing only for his inside pass to fail to find a man. South Africa hacked the ball downfield and the Lions conceded a penalty.

A week earlier and such an opportunity would have been squandered. But not this time. Janie de Beer had replaced Henry Honiball at outside half and he is a man who can kick a goal – which he did with some aplomb. De Beer scored another penalty and then, after 17 minutes, the Springboks scored

might have been. For if the Free State outside-half had been in the No 10 shirt a week earlier South Africa may well have been contesting this Test on equal footing with their visitors.

Now it was the turn of the Lions to enjoy some success as the architect of the Second Test triumph, Neil Jenkins, hit superb form again. He was to have fours shots at goal all afternoon – and he found the target every time. Three successive penalties brought the Lions back into the match so that at half time it stood at 13-9 to the home side.

When Jenkins kicked his first goal he want past 100 points for the tour and by the time the afternoon was over, his total of 41 points from three matches was the best-ever for a player in the Tests on a Lions tour.

But if the Lions thought they could re-group at half-time (when Jeremy Guscott left the battle with a broken arm to be replaced by Allan Bateman) they were to get a shock within three minutes of the

second-half starting when the Springboks scored another try – Joost van der Westhuizen wriggling and snaking his way past the tackle of his opposite number, Matt Dawson, then Allan Bateman before finding the line. De Beer's conversion made it 20-9 and the Springboks were threatening to run away with it.

Before the tour started the key battle and one of the most fascinating duels was always going to be between van der Westhuizen and Robert Howley. The fact that Howley never reached the Test matches because of injury was seen as catastrophic blow to the Lions' hopes. His replacement Dawson, however, played out of his skin and matched van der Westhuizen step-for-step.

So it was no surprise that Dawson should score his second Test try in three matches as the Lions gave themselves a last chance of victory and the clean sweep. It came from another stirring performance

their first try of the match when Percy Montgomery made the touch down with men outside him waiting for the pass had he run into trouble. Up stepped de Beer – two more points and a lead of 13-0. With every swing of his boot de Beer was warming Springbok hearts and tolling a lament for what

from the visitors' pack aided and abetted by the scything running of Bateman and John Bentley. Holes were made in the Springbok defence, Tom Smith the prop set up the first of a series of rucks. The ball popped up and Martin Johnson delivered the pass to Dawson. Another dummy, a dart and a

Boiling point... tempers flare in the Third Test (opposite left). Tony Underwood's Lions debut ends prematurely while (below) the bloody scars of battle for Springbok prop Adrian Garvey

stretch and it was a try. Jenkins converted it.

The Lions were back in it, looking as if they could score again while knowing that any slip and another try for South Africa would mean defeat. The two packs which had virtually fought themselves to a stand still – and literally in the first half when the punches started to fly – stirred themselves for one last titanic effort.

Throughout this match the Lions saw more of the ball in the backs than the other two games combined. Catt tried to be creative, threw long flat passes and generally prodded without great success for an opening. There were one or two chances which came and went and but for the wrong option being picked, the poor pass being hurled to a space where there was no man, the end result might have been so different. Even so it was the Lions who

were in the ascendency when they were hit by two late, late tries. The damage was done by the winger Pieter Rossouw who first drew the defence with an angled run and passed to Andre Snyman. Then with three minutes left Rossouw scored a splendid solo try of his own. That made it 35-16 – game to the Springboks, series to the Lions.

It had been a stirring encounter and the Lions had rumbled with menacing intent during long periods of the second half. But where as on the other two Saturdays of Test match action they had been able to deliver the telling blow when it mattered most, this time it went awry at the crucial moment. Even so, the final whistle marked the end of an historic series and for the impartial, a justice of sorts. South Africa had saved some face and the Lions were

Rob Wainwright feels the full force of Springbok rucking while (top right) Paul Wallace takes on the South Africa defence in Johannesburg. Friends for life...(right) John Bentley embraces Neil Jenkins

covered in glory. McGeechan had it all in perspective when he said: "The job was to win the Test series and we've done that. We also produced a high quality Test match to finish." Martin Johnson, the successful Lions skipper, collected a giant trophy and the Lions, the players and substitutes for the day, the rest of the squad in blazers on the bench, came down to the field to celebrate in style, making sure to do a victory lap and salute the barmy army. There was even spontaneous praise from their rivals. Van der Westhuizen, who had taken over the captaincy during the match when Gary Teichmann went off injured, said: "We learned a lot from them, their handling skills and the way they took the ball forward surprised us."

Johnson, who was returning home for an operation, said: "The Springboks deserved their victory because they played better than us and I have no problems with that. We had a chance of victory after fighting back to 23-16 and had the ball in their 22, but didn't take the opportunity.

"We couldn't pull it off, but I was proud to lift the trophy and it was the culmination of a great squad effort. There hasn't been anyone in this party who has let anyone down. This match proved how good the Springboks are and how superb our defence has been in the first two Tests to keep them out."

The British Isles party were in no doubt that the tour had been more than worthwhile. "I had forgotten how enjoyable it was working with internationals," said McGeechan. "We talk about a whole team effort and in that respect it was probably the best tour I have ever been on."

High on their achievements, and deservedly so, the Lions had earned a place in the game's hall of fame, won respect for Northern hemisphere rugby and even prompted McGeechan to call for them to reunite sooner rather than later to keep the standard rising. "We must be careful not to accept the Five Nations as our top level – in terms of world rugby it is not and these players have benefitted from being together for two months and playing at a higher level than they experience at home."

That final whistle at Ellis Park should have signalled the

end of a long season – yet for a number of the Englishmen in the party there was another long flight looming and one more match – for England against Australia in Sydney – a game that these tired men playing in a disjointed side were to lose 25-6.

"I'm very tired and this has been a long season for everyone involved in the Lions," said Johnson and he wasn't even going down under.

But back to the glory and the sheer buzz and pleasure of it all. It was, and will be, a tour to relish for years and years to come, a trip made of memories to be enjoyed on many a long winter evening. "The sadness for me is we will touch down in London, shake hands and the 1997 Lions will be gone forever," said McGeechan. Magic always has had that ephemeral quality – and the 1997 Lions tour, shaped by hard work and profound thinking, was certainly overflowing with it – the boys of the British Isles and Ireland were absolutely magic.

TEN

Lions in **Union**

BODIES ached and the final Test was lost. But as the Lions huddled together one voice chanted out their immense achievement. "Two-one, two-one, two-one," roared John Bentley. This day the final Test had gone to the Boks but the series belonged to the Lions. And Bentley wasn't going to let anyone forget it.

The informed experts said it couldn't be done, the bookies – never generous at the best of times – were offering 5-1 on them to lose all three Tests and the rugby-mad South Africans were relishing the prospect of a handsome triumph.

Yet the party of 35 Lions – made up of Scots, Irish, Welsh and English – formed a bond, a brotherhood which would not be breached on the field and which will remain powerful and exclusive throughout their lives.

This was a special group of men united by rugby and totally focused on winning in South Africa, a hostile land of tough, uncompromising players born to win and driven by the weight of historical expectation.

It may not have been a war, but the words of Winston Churchill in 1940 had a real relevance to that Lions party of 1997: "Victory at all costs ... victory however long and hard the road."

Indeed. It was that Churchillian spirit which meant this was a victory for every man who wore the famous red shirt. Every contribution counted and every man ended up a hero.

A philosophy of "All for one, and one for all" never worked better. This was a real pride of Lions.

> 'This was a special effort by the squad. We hung on in there, kicked goals, kept tackling, kept believing'
> – Lawrence Dallaglio

In My View

By Colin Price, Rugby Correspondent of The Mirror

> 'Jenkins' trick with an orange brought the house down – just as his five penalties set up the Boks for Guscott's winner'

IT was a bleary-eyed morning after the glorious night before as Neil Jenkins wobbled uncertainly into the team hotel located right on Durban's teeming seafront. As the incredible Welsh points-scoring machine picked his way cautiously through the human debris still scattered around the marble foyer, one of the Indian waiters spotted that unmistakable carrot top. "Mr Jenkins, Mr Jenkins," he exclaimed. "You are a wonderful ball kicker. It is an honour to speak to you." Whereupon the full-back whose dead-eye place kicking had earned the 1997 Lions the glory of becoming only the second side this century to win a Test series in South Africa, launched into an hilarious action replay of the sight that will give the Boks nightmares for years to come.

Reaching out for an orange from the huge breakfast fruit bowl, Jenks plonked it down on the shiny marble floor and went painstakingly through his entire time-consuming repertoire...

Three long striding half-moon steps to the left ... hands held busily out at his side ... the deepest of breaths ... a constant re-assuring glance at the imaginary target above ... and then, somehow, he manages to put it all together in a clearly scrambled brain and send the orange sailing perfectly into orbit over the breakfast table.

It brought the house down – just as it had hours earlier when a sea of replica red jerseys looked to have turned the magnificent King's Park stadium into the green, green grass of home as five Jenkins' penalties set up the Springboks perfectly for Jeremy Guscott's winning drop goal.

Modestly he reflected on his achievements of the evening before: "I am there to do a job and all I kept imagining was being on the practice ground. I managed to block the crowd out and put the kicks over. It was a huge day. I've experienced some real hidings from South Africa games with Wales so it has been a great achievement to come through and win the series."

How different from the scenes of wreckage and mayhem that studded Willie-John McBride's conquering Lions celebrations back in 1974. Though current manager Fran Cotton was a bulwark prop and coach Ian McGeechan a magical centre of the '74 side, it was a completely different world even then. No praise

Man of Steel... Neil Jenkins, whose impromptu demonstration proved he's the jaffa when it comes to kicking!

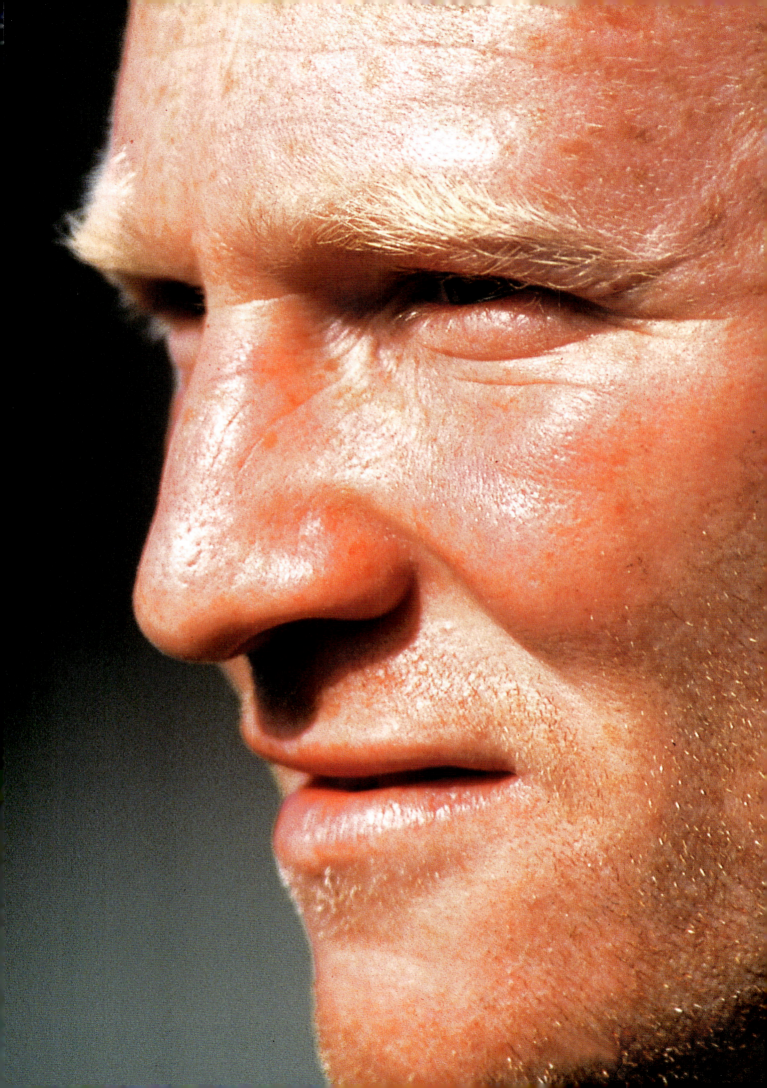

Scott Gibbs took the South Africans on at their own game, tackling the biggest first — and with the biggest hits

can be too high, no tributes more deserved than for Martin Johnson's unfancied side as they wrote their names into rugby folklore. Yes, I too predicted seven weeks of misery ahead for a knackered squad as they left their Weybridge headquarters after a crucial week of bonding and headed off to South Africa. The appointment of the abrasive Johnson and Cotton's pledge that "this side will not take a single step backwards," was misinterpreted over there as an act of rugby warfare.

The Lions were coming to punch and kick their way around South Africa just as Willie-John's team had done 23 years earlier with its infamous "99 call", a shout to get your retaliation in before the opponents have thought about hitting you.

Instead the Lions captivated their hard-bitten hosts by storming through the provinces with some sublime rugby football. The "midweek" team, especially, put together a set of massive victories to ensure huge headaches at selection meetings and a massive boost for the "Saturday" side.

More importantly, it forged a collective iron spirit among the players drawn from four patriotic national teams – a spirit that ultimately saw them through amazing pressure in Test matches when the dazzling Lions found no room to cut loose.

First at Cape Town and then in Durban, the series was won on monster tackling. If powerhouse centre Scott Gibbs struck the psychological hits by blitzing the biggest targets he could find, the back row of Lawrence Dallaglio, Tim Rodber and Richard Hill were immense.

That, and the Boks' arrogant decision to go into the First Test without a recognised goalkicker, enabled the Lions to paper over huge cracks and take their place in history.

The Lions never quite got to grips with the Boks' mighty scrummaging power so, wisely, they threw two mobile props, in Tom Smith and Paul Wallace, at them. Jenkins, for all his wonderfully accurate goalkicking, was no full-back. Yet it took South Africa three Tests to pick a fly-half capable of torturing him out of position.

The Lions made up for the potentially crippling blows of losing world-class scrum-half Rob Howley by drawing the best out of Matt Dawson, whose one-handed dummy virtually won the Cape Town Test. And when Ieuan Evans limped home to leave the team without its only class flier, tour talisman John Bentley came in to become the first man to play for Britain at both rugby codes. Bentos, whose brilliant solo try against Gauteng Lions had more than any other single factor got the tour back on track after the only provincial defeat by Northern Transvaal, had deficiencies. But even when his missed tackle let in Andre Joubert for a potentially

disastrous try at Durban, Bentley disarmed everyone by admitting: "I was looking round for a shovel to dig a bloody great hole for myself."

By the end of the tour, McGeechan was looking like the crop-haired Bentley. His straggly locks snipped away by another of the tour characters, Irish hooker Keith Wood, to honour a promise he made if the Lions won the series.

Only the horrendous injury list and the mental switch-off after winning the series saved Cotton from going the same way for a first-ever clean sweep in the final one-sided Test at Ellis Park.

Alas, that proved to be a game too far for these fantastic tourists. But by then, unlike McGeechan, we'd all let our hair down.

At times, the Players Court was a more dangerous place to be than the bottom of any Springbok-trampled ruck. Poor Bentley had painful memories of Brisbane on his first England tour nine years earlier when, for the crime of being young and lively, he was tied to a tree outside a restaurant and forced to sing a French love-song every five minutes.

Right at the end, the then-England captain John Orwin crept up and poured a pint of beer on his head. This time Richmond's new hooker Barry Williams found himself in the chair during a wild afternoon of celebration at the sponsors' party on the day before the Lions flew home. To mark his 23rd birthday, the Wales hooker was stripped to his underpants and trussed to a chair – but, as the only Welshman who can't sing, his team-mates gagged him rather than spoil the wailing tunes of Oasis.

Shutting motormouth Austin Healey up was an almost impossible task – until shaven-headed Lord Justice Keith Wood ordered him to stand in a corner with an apple wedged and taped into his mouth. Close friends swore it was the first time he had been quiet for more than 30 seconds – even in his sleep.

Jeremy Guscott came to regret a flippant throw-away line to Alan Tait as he sat out yet another training session through injury. "Hello Alan, are you still on tour?" asked Guscott mischievously.

Two weeks later, Guscott was leaping on the Scotsman's back after Tait scored the winning try in the First Test at Cape Town.

But the quote of the tour came from Scotland captain Rob Wainwright as England's specially-chartered flying cigar plane hit turbulence and plunged hundreds of feet in an air-pocket on the flight back from Bloemfontein.

In his best Private Fraser accent, he cried: "We're all doooomed". By then, of course, it was the Springboks who were doomed.

David Young and Scott
Gibbs swap notes with
former Lions scrum-
half Gareth Edwards

Backstage Aces

WHEN players are wrenched away from home and family for two arduous months of the most intense rugby of their careers, the last thing they want to worry about is their itinerary, hotels and where the next clean pair of shorts are coming from.

Everything from training sessions to making sure everybody is on the connecting flight must be planned to the last second – all the players need do is worry about their performance on the pitch. A successful squad must be molly-coddled by the backroom staff at every turn, lovingly nurtured and generally spoilt and pampered throughout.

That the 1997 British Lions were so clearly focused on their game must therefore be seen as a glowing tribute to the 10 men and one woman who worked tirelessly in making rugby history happen. From manager Fran Cotton downwards, there was a constant hive of activity behind the scenes rewarded with a Test series victory and all swept before them bar Northern Transvaal.

Success begins at the top and Cotton stamped his own inimitable style on the tour from the word go when, in February, he announced a provisional 62-man squad. It was clear from the outset that the former England prop was going to do things his own way. A veteran of three Lions' tours as a player, perhaps Cotton's greatest achievement was his ability to create a strong sense of unity amongst his team, casting aside traditional domestic rivalries to create an unprecedented sense of purpose. The real masterstroke

in man-management was to make all the players believe they were capable of making the Test side and that had two profound effects on the party.

It got the best out of everybody in the provincial matches. Nobody was allowed to rest on their laurels or think that an honour-strewn international career would influence selection. In Cotton's eyes a player was only as good as his last match. In leaving the door open to all, he averted any repeat of the splintering which plagued the latter parts of the 1993 Lions tour to New Zealand. On that tour the shape of the Test side was determined early on, meaning those left out felt as if they were only there to make up the numbers. The cause and effect – animosity between the two sets of players which consequently caused their performances on the pitch to suffer.

In South Africa in 1997 it was so different. All the players had a chance, right up to the final Test in Johannesburg and, as a consequence, they worked selflessly for each other. Cotton had achieved what historically had been virtually impossible, he had blended the disparate groups of Englishmen, Scots, Irish and Welsh into one powerful unit.

The manager won the respect of his players because they knew he would look after them. After Doddie Weir was brutally kicked by the Mpumalanga lock Marius Bosman, prematurely ending the Scottish lock's tour, Cotton was livid. "My priority is to ensure the Lions are properly protected," he said.

Then, when after the match against Western Province, John Bentley was accused of eye-gouging in the South African press by Springbok winger James Small, Cotton asked the Newcastle man if there was any truth in the reports. Bentley said no and Cotton took him at his word, steadfastly defending his man against the barrage of accusations.

While Cotton was the gnarled, no-nonsense figurehead, Ian McGeechan, the Lions coach,

Plenty to ponder for Fran
Cotton and (opposite) his
chief coach Ian McGeechan

was the quiet, unassuming master tactician content
to ply his trade on the training ground and let the
players put it into practice on the pitch. The
Northampton Director of Rugby has now completed
five Lions tours as player and coach, but the former
Scotland fly-half-cum-centre would be hard pushed
to top the success he achieved with the 1997 Lions
in South Africa.

His speciality is the backs and McGeechan performed something of a miracle by transforming
traditionally stilted British three-quarters into quick-
thinking, exciting and incisive world-beaters. Not
only that, he taught them how to win in style.

The South Africans were astounded by the way
the Lions ran the ball at almost every opportunity,
taking up previously alien lines of running and, at
times, cutting the best defences to shreds. The home
sides became progressively more terrified of this
threat out wide and their inability to combat the
danger led to panic. McGeechan had harnessed the
talent at his disposal and in the process made northern hemisphere players perform like their southern
hemisphere counterparts. In every match on tour,
the Lions backs were a revelation. In the past British
sides have tried to play a more expansive game,
but none have managed to come anywhere near the
fluidity and penetration that McGeechan achieved.

McGeechan also succeeded in strengthening players'
apparent weaknesses. By the end of the tour few
critics were still sniping about Tony Underwood's
defensive qualities, many were praising Neil Jenkins
previously questionable positional sense and the
plaudits for Matt Dawson – perceived as the weak
link only weeks before – were gushing.

The wily old campaigner had done a marvellous
job. For not only had the Lions backs produced the
kind of rugby which we had previously seen in the
Super-12s, they were playing effective, winning
rugby. McGeechan had proved the British could
really play.

However McGeechan would be the first to
acknowledge the contribution of his fellow Scot Jim
Telfer, the forwards coach. Both men know glittering
displays like those witnessed in South Africa cannot
be achieved without a solid foundation and Telfer
was the man to provide it. The war of attrition
waged up front by the Lions forwards, orchestrated
by Telfer, was not always pretty and not always as
commanding as they would have liked, but without
their efforts there would have been none of the
pyrotechnics out wide.

There is no tougher, rougher, more intimidating
destination on the rugby map than South Africa –
not even New Zealand – and Telfer made certain his

men were ready for the most physical examination of their careers. His big success was finding the right balance between dynamic, open play in the forwards – which was central to the Lions' overall game plan – and a good old-fashioned bit of donkey work up front.

Telfer instilled a work ethic which carried the team through some of the stickiest moments of the tour. When his front five struggled against Western Province, prompting predictions that the Lions front row would be murdered in the Tests, Telfer refused to panic or look for scapegoats. Instead he convened extra scrummaging sessions which made impartial observers wince at the ferocity of them, but he got the problem sorted. His reward was to sit in the stands of the Newlands Stadium in Cape Town during the First Test and watch as the Springboks failed to shunt the Lions pack off the pitch. His men held firm and Telfer could be satisfied that the extra hours on the training ground had been worth every last drop of sweat and gasped breath.

Under Telfer's steely eye a number of Lions forwards excelled on tour, surpassing perhaps even their own expectations of their capabilities – and none more so than Neil Back. The Leicester openside blossomed under Telfer's tutelage – himself an abrasive, rampaging flanker for Scotland and the Lions – and added dimensions to his play which ultimately earned him a place in the starting line-up for the Third Test. Most noticeable was Back's body position in the tackle. He had always been dynamic, but now he had found the ability to go in lower and drive even the biggest and most powerful South Africans backwards.

Others flourished under the Scot's guidance. Eric Miller, Back's Leicester team-mate, went on tour as a highly-promising youngster, but came home a fully-fledged international No 8.

Similarly the two Test props – Scotland's Tom Smith and Ireland's Paul Wallace – also returned to Britain better players. Telfer worked miracles with both men and they responded whole-heartedly. But the Cotton, McGeechan and Telfer triumvirate were not the only ones on the management side to make a big impact. Technical coaching assistant Andy Keast did much to shape the Lions' play and his understanding of South African rugby – having helped Natal to victory in the 1995 Currie Cup – was fundamental in the way that the squad approached each game. A former Metropolitan Police and Middlesex coach now with Harlequins, Keast exploited all of his local knowledge during the tour.

One of the happiest men on tour must have been the Lions' fitness adviser Dave McLean, who helped produce the most durable Lions team of the modern era. Game after game the Lions finished stronger than the opposition to either hammer home their advantage or snatch victory from the jaws of defeat.

A late addition to the Lions' backroom staff was kicking guru Dave Aldred, but he proved himself a worthy member of the team with the emergence of Tim Stimpson as world-class place-kicker. Aldred was central to the Newcastle full-back's progress as a first-choice kicker, dispelling doubts about his ability at the highest level. Stimpson finished the tour as the leading points-scorer with 111 and Aldred can rightly claim some credit.

The three busiest men in South Africa were the medical officer, Dr James Robson, physiotherapist Mark Davies and masseur Richard Wegrzyk, who at times must have felt like they were fighting a losing battle as wounded Lion after wounded Lion needed running repairs. South Africa's hard grounds and even harder players certainly took their toll on the squad, but collectively Robson, Davies and Wegrzyk kept them going long enough to complete the tour.

The remaining three people behind the scenes may not have ventured on to the training pitch but their contribution was no less significant.

Baggage master Stan Bagshaw, press officer Bob Burrows, Chief Executive of Bedford, and administrative assistant Sam Peters – a cigarette smoker in a land of no smokers – all worked wonders to ensure that the first-ever professional Lions tour was the smoothest and most thoroughly organised in Lions' history.

THIRTEEN

Golden Moments

WHAT shocked the South Africans most: the fact the British Lions actually won the Test series or the style in which they played? There can have been few outside of the inner sanctum who could have imagined just how dynamic, incisive and simply exciting the Lions could be. Between them Fran Cotton, Ian McGeechan and Jim Telfer transformed players accustomed to percentage rugby into a scintillating unit capable of thrilling, fluid and adventurous rugby.

For years the French have had the monopoly on exciting, free-flowing rugby in the Northern hemisphere. The four Home Unions have had their moments, but never convincingly emulating the flair of their Gallic neighbours – until now. And that is why the Lions produced so many golden moments. The tries they scored, at an average of over four per game, were invariably the result of sweeping moves rather than trundling forward drives.

The most spectacular score of the tour came in the sixth match against Gauteng when one man decided he would temporarily abandon the Lions' new-found code of interactive, 15-man rugby and have a go himself. Exactly why John Bentley thought he was capable of taking on almost the entire Gauteng side single-handedly remains a mystery, but the end product was so electrifying that it hardly mattered as he powered into the final five metres, dragging two

desperate Gauteng defenders with him across the line.

The Newcastle winger had collected the ball deep inside his own half from a Neil Jenkins' pass after an aimless clearance by the home side. Only 15 supercharged South Africans and a mere 70 yards stood between him and glory. It was no great surprise when he beat the first two would-be tacklers – both forwards – but as he built up speed there was palpable panic spreading through the Gauteng ranks. At this point, however, Bentley appeared to take the wrong option, cutting inside rather than moving the ball wide to Jeremy Guscott.

If Guscott felt disappointed about the apparent snub, his animosity would have been short-lived as he watched Bentley find an extra change of pace which took him scorching through the heart of the defence and over for a sensational score that is as fresh in the memory now as it was moments after it happened.

What made Bentley's effort even more satisfying – if that was possible – was the timing. The Lions had struggled throughout the match and were in danger of crashing to a morale-sapping second successive defeat until his wonderful intervention. Later Bentley modestly tried to talk down his efforts: "The try was the icing on the cake of a superb team performance which turned the tour around after our defeat against Northern Transvaal.

Prize jaws... Lions at play on the golf course and at the barbecue

But I don't think we should go on about it all night." Fran Cotton simply described it as a "defining moment" of the tour.

The only other moment on the tour which compares as an encapsulated snapshot of high drama came in the First Test in Cape Town and involved the unlikeliest of heroes – Northampton's Matt Dawson. Many thought Dawson shouldn't have been on the tour. He had had an injury-plagued season and was England's fourth choice scrum-half, yet by the time the Lions' came home he had made his detractors eat their words.

In Cape Town the team was trailing 16-15, the minutes were ticking by and it looked as though the Lions were destined to fill their allotted place in the canon of British sport – glorious, gallant losers. Mercifully nobody had told Dawson that the script was already written as he set out to carve himself an enduring place in rugby folklore.

It happened like this. The Lions had a scrum on the Springbok's 22 metre line and after a clean strike from Keith Wood, the ball rested at Tim Rodber's feet. The question was simple – how would the Lions finally break down what had been an impenetrable South African defensive wall? The answer was Dawson. Picking up from the base, the Northampton No 9 scampered down the blindside, evading the tackle of Ruben Kruger and keeping fractionally ahead of the pursuing Joost van der Westhuizen.

It was a smart break, but with Andre Joubert, Gary Teichmann and Andre Venter zeroing in on the smallest Lions player on the pitch, the time had come to move the ball back to the forwards and think again. But again nobody had told Dawson this was the plan.

Seemingly cornered, Dawson lifted his arms as if to pass the ball, basketball-style, over the heads of the defence. His Michael Jordan impression could not have confused the Springboks more and they hesitated for a split second, anticipating the marauding Lions backrow charging up in support. While they checked, Dawson carried serenely on to the line for a try which silenced the crowd, left the Springbok players staring at each other in disbelief and started the kind of celebrations among the 6,000 or so Lions fans in the Newlands stadium usually reserved for New Years Eve parties and royal weddings. "I always believed in my ability to play on the world stage if only I could play in the

Tests," a delighted Dawson said after the match. "I always had my heart set on the Lions tour."

But what made the try even more magical was the way it symbolised the Lions' refusal to be bowed by the Springboks. For more than an hour the Lions had weathered the South African onslaught but had still kept within striking distance of their opponents.

When Dawson scored, the look on the Springbok players' faces said it all. They just could not believe the Lions were capable of absorbing all that pressure and could still come back to snatch the lead. No team had ever done this to them before.

There were other great tries which may not have had quite the same impact as Dawson's but, in their own way, were just as enthralling. Probably the most symbolic were the three Rob Wainwright scored in the Mpumalanga match and it was a shame for the Scotland skipper that the kick which ended Doddie Weir's tour grabbed the headlines.

It was not just the speed of his scores, which came in a record nine-minute burst, it was the attacking rugby which lead to his hat-trick which was the most satisfying as the Lions cut loose with the kind of attacking rugby we had only previously dreamed about.

There were four hat-tricks and the most applauded was probably Nick Beal's against the Emerging Springboks. The versatile Northampton and England player was a consistent and unflinching performer and his three tries won him the man-of-the-match vote. Beal was irrepressible on the left wing and all of his tries were classic examples of pace, power and intelligent support.

However there were more than tries to celebrate. Take Scott Gibbs' tackling. The Swansea powerhouse never flinched and put in some of the biggest hits that you are ever likely see in international rugby. Even the indomitable Tim Rodber would have to concede the title of the squad's hardest hit-man to the Welsh centre.

Gibbs was fearless. Be it a 20-stone prop or a mere centre charging towards him, the result was invariably the same – the ball-carrier going backwards at a rate of knots, often with an uncomprehending expression written all over his face. Perhaps the most shuddering, bone-crunching

Family favourite... an airport reunion for tour hero Jeremy Guscott from wife Jane, daughters Holly 2, Imogen 4, and baby Saskia

Vintage years... Ian McGeechan, Martin Johnson and Fran Cotton triumphant. Willie-John McBride (right) savours the moment of triumph with his all-conquering 1974 Lions

tackle came in the First Test in Cape Town when Springbok winger Andre Snyman took the almost suicidal decision to run at Gibbs and was almost immediately made to regret his folly. With a firm grip around the Northern Transvaal man's legs, the Welshman put all of his 15 stone 7 pound bulk into the hit and sent him reeling backwards with such force it is debatable whether Snyman knew what was happening. Subsequent analysis of the tackle on video has estimated the two players impacted at around 40 mph.

Another who left an indelible mark on the tour was Neil Back who played the best rugby of his career in South Africa and it was fitting tribute to his efforts that he was selected for the Third Test in Johannesburg on merit. Finally, the Leicester open-side had been given the recognition he had worked so hard for. It was the tour of the little big man.

From the moment he stepped on the pitch for his first game in South Africa, against Border, Back was virtually unstoppable. With a new-found defensive steel to his game, he looked like the complete No 7 and was far from embarrassed by his bigger, stronger opponents. Saracen's Richard Hill edged him out for a place in the first two Tests but Back continued to push his claim and in the end Cotton could not ignore it. In a world of giants who

are getting yet bigger and bigger, the diminutive Back had proved himself worthy of his place.

The final mention, however, must go to the legion of boisterous but good-humoured British Lions whose vocal support and colourful antics were a feature of the tour from day one. At every match the Lions fans, Union Jacks draped around their shoulders and their faces daubed with war paint, were there to cheer on the team and revel in the victories. As the weeks passed so their numbers swelled and an abiding memory is the sound of 'Swing Low, Sweet Chariot' reverberating around the Newlands stadium after the Lions had taken the lead through Dawson, followed by a stunned silence from the Springbok fans.

Francois Pienaar, the Springboks' deposed World Cup-winning captain, said he had never encountered such fanatical, passionate fans and recalled how a group of Lions supporters drowned out a bar after the Second Test with two hours of uninterrupted singing.

Yes, the Lions in South Africa was a magical time for everybody involved and you would have been hard-pushed to write a better script for the two-month adventure. They played exciting rugby, they won matches and they clinched the Test series. Who could have dared hope for more?

A Place in History

GREAT, greater, greatest ... what place the Lions of '97 in the pantheon of rugby history? The record book puts this '97 party of apparent no-hopers up there with the gods of the game because they were winners in a land where angels and even New Zealanders sometimes fear to tread – and how they deserve their place!

Yet bald statistics only give a half-measure of the true impact of the side, factors of time and place play just as important a role. As a true measure of the achievements of the 1997 Lions consider this. The dwindling years of the 20th century have coincided with a dramatic reshaping of the game that has made the upheaval of the industrial revolution seem positively pedestrian. Professionalism, world cups, super 12s, European Cups and, after more

than 100 years of feuding, rugby union and rugby league embracing one another like long-lost lovers rather than blood enemies.

Against this background the concept of Lions rugby seemed an anachronism and, indeed, for it to survive as a viable concept, success in South Africa was probably imperative. The tour, as ever, may have been rooted in tradition, but there was one major concession to the new order – the players became the first-ever paid Lions. It was not a king's ransom, but it was a move in the right direction.

Yet money alone could not act as the sole motivation for a party of men bent on upsetting a world pecking order established by three world cups which had been under complete southern hemisphere domination. New Zealand took the first title in 1987, Australia did it in 1991 and South Africa in 1995. On top of that, tours by those three nations to face the Home Unions and France had, by and large, served to emphasis the superiority of the south.

So, from the evidence of the 1997 Home International championship and from there an appraisal of the Lions squad, the South African hosts waited with glee for the first British Isles tour to their shores in 17 years. Rugby is everything to South Africans and always, but always, takes top billing. Where else could news that rain threatened to water-log a rugby ground become the main item on front pages while a plot to kill President Nelson Mandela merited a brief mention at the bottom of the page?

The concept of defeat is also alien to South African minds and so the locals waited, building up an appetite ready to gorge on a glorious Test victory which they considered an enticing certainty. The Springboks may have been beaten at home by New Zealand in 1996, but no South African side had ever lost back-to-back home series – and certainly not against the likes of the Lions.

There were eight provincial games before the First Test and the Lions made a less than convincing start at Port Elizabeth against Eastern Province. The Lions had their moments in the tour opener, but lacked continuity. It got a bit better as they went along as wins over Border, Western Province and Mpumalanga (formerly South East Transvaal) proved. But then the Lions lost 35-30 to Northern Transvaal and with just three matches before the First Test at Cape Town those preconceived notions that they were ripe for the picking surfaced. The Springboks

were looking forward to a feast. The key players for the home side had been withdrawn from their provincial sides in anticipation of that First Test and they had trained long and hard and were ready to make it count at Cape Town.

Adversity, however, is the pal of many underdogs and Martin Johnson's team forged a bond that transcended historical squabbles and grudges that characterise the relationship between England, Scotland, Wales and Ireland. These men, all 35 of them, were there to stand united and, if it came to it, fall united.

Victory in the First Test at Cape Town meant that the Lions headed for Durban knowing that they had two chances to clinch a series win – something that had last been achieved by Willie-John McBride's legendary 1974 team which won 21 of 22 games and drew one match. Johnson's priority was to keep his team believing in themselves, to maintain the momentum and to meet the expected onslaught with the most resolute of resolute defences. The team for that June 28 Durban match more than did that. The tackling was out of this world and when Jerry Guscott dropped a late goal to make it 18-15 to the visitors, the Lions had made a mockery of conventional wisdom.

Game and series to the Lions with one match to go. Johnson had entered the halls of the rugby hallowed as the first Englishman of the modern era to lead a Lions side to such a milestone. Indeed his name can now be mentioned in the same breath as the Scotsman Finlay Calder (victorious in Australia in 1989), the Irishman Willie-John McBride, and the Welshman John Dawes (a 2-1 series win in New Zealand in 1970).

Pride, determination, no shortage of underrated skill allied to a telling sense of purpose had earned Johnson and his Lions, every single one of them, a place in the sport's legend book. Through the history of the Lions, pride has driven teams to greatness, pride in themselves, in the famous red shirt and in the winning.

And it has always been just so from the first tour by a team to carry the name the British Lions. A lion motif on a tie gave the best of British rugby its roar back in 1924 when the Lions first headed for South Africa on a mission of conquest and conversion and with a history of having lost just four of 13 internationals against their hosts.

The record, however, was to be dented this time as the four-match Test series ended with three defeats and a draw. The whole tour brought a paltry nine wins from 21 matches and marked the start of an era that saw the Lions go until 1938 before their next win in South Africa.

Even so, 73 years on and the Lions survive as the team at the pinnacle of the British game, the diverse roots of the side's beginnings having survived and, in light of Johnson's success, flourished against the years of upheaval including professionalism.

The first overseas tour of any sorts was in 1888 when a Great Britain team played in Australia and over the years, to 1910, various tours took place under that banner but were never representative. The 1891 Great Britain party to South Africa consisted of just English and Scots.

The breakthrough was in 1910 when a proper representative British Isles team was sent out and by 1924 the side was selected, not invited. The Lions as we know them today were in place, but had been playing in all but name for the previous 14 years. 1910 is regarded as the year the British Isles team was born.

But first it is worth going back to 1888 when R L Seddon, one of three English cricketers who had toured Australia the previous year, thought a rugby trip down under would go down a treat. The idea was enthusiastically embraced and those tourists went on the longest rugby trek in history – 74 matches spread over 18 months.

In that time Seddon was killed, drowned on a trip to Hunter River in New South Wales and Andrew Stoddart, the Blackheath and Middlesex player, stepped into the breach.

Three years later came that trip made by the Englishmen and Scots – the first tour of South Africa – and they went on an unbeaten run that stretched for a total of 19 games including the first game against South Africa, at Port Elizabeth, which ended in a 4-0 win for the British Isles. But the balance of power was changing as the game was introduced around the world – frequently through the ports of call for the navy.

Today, in spite of some epic series, the official figures have South Africa winning 19 out of 33 matches with four draws – and perhaps that goes a long way towards explaining why 1997 has been so special.

It is the same story for the Lions in New Zealand, another popular destination, where the record is even worse – 23 defeats, six wins and two draws and just one series victory. Only Australia fall to the Lions on anything like a regular basis. They have won two of the ten games against the British tourists.

Lions tours though are few and far between, making the record 17 caps won by McBride between 1962-74 remarkable. The giant Ireland lock also played 15 consecutive games and captained the side to arguably their finest series win on the 1974 tour of South Africa. That roll-call for caps won helps explain why the Lions concept has maintained its mystique. A cap for the British Isles is precious indeed and the currency has retained its value. The last Lions tour was four years ago – a 2-1 defeat in New Zealand, meaning a grand total of 45 caps awarded. The use of replacements and substitutes has raised the number of caps available, but still they are prized possessions that will never be easy to win. Think of poor Robert Howley, the outstanding Wales scrum half and a certain Test player. Injury robbed him of his cap and it will be four years before he has another chance. In sport four years is a lifetime and more.

Weeks away from home can take its toll, even when the trip is going well and the Lions are no strangers to controversy. The 1930 tour to New Zealand managed by James "Bim" Baxter ended in a huge row and emphatic defeat for the British Isles after Baxter complained about the way New Zealand employed their wing-forward, a player involved in a very different way to the wing-forward of today. Back then the scrums were two-three-two with the wing-forward standing just off the bound-on players and ready to cause havoc. Baxter was so irritated by what he saw that he accused the New Zealand wing-forward of being a "cheat". No wonder the Lions lost with the hosts' sensibilities stirred up by this remark – yet Baxter was to have the last word. A member of the law-making International Rugby Board, Baxter was able to lobby for a rule change and as a consequence, two years later, the front row had to consist of three players.

Then in 1938 Sam Walker, the Ireland captain, led a tour to South Africa, which was to be the last for 12 years because of the Second World War, but absence seemed to make the heart grow fonder.

Another Irishman, Karl Mullen, was captain on the return of the British Isles in 1950. That tour was to New Zealand and Australia. The Lions drew the First Test against New Zealand 9-9, but lost the next three. In Australia they redressed the balance with two emphatic victories.

Immensely popular tourists, these Lions were the first to wear the famous kit that we know today – the red shirts, white shorts, dark blue socks with emerald tops – a neat amalgamation of the colours of the home nations.

The party to South Africa in 1955 was led by yet another Irishman, Robin Thompson, the Instonians, London Irish and Ireland forward. Rated one of the strongest-ever British Isles' teams, the series was a thriller with the Lions taking the first Test 23-22. They lost the second, won the third, but saw the fourth slip as they went down 22-8 and ended up sharing the series. This was the tour that saw the likes of Cliff Morgan and Clem

Thomas make a big impact. The team was still highly-rated when it went to New Zealand in 1959, but the forwards lacked enough power and the Lions lost 3-1. The gulf between the northern and southern hemispheres was widening as the British Isles tried to turn the emphasis of their rugby to forward power. It didn't work. The 1960s were grim times indeed as three tours – 12 Tests – resulted in no wins and two draws. The credibility of the whole Lions ethos was under pressure, but a shift to absolute commitment and efficient safety-first rugby was to turn the tide.

The 1971 Lions went to New Zealand led by the first Welshman to become British Isles captain, John Dawes, and coached by Carwyn James. The four-Test series was stunning with the British Isles winning 9-3 in Dunedin, losing in Christchurch and winning in Wellington. The fourth and final match in Auckland was a 14-14 draw and the Lions had scored a remarkable victory that had their hosts stunned. In 1974 McBride's legendary Lions went to South Africa and won the four-Test series 3-0 with one match drawn as the Lions enjoyed their golden days.

Yet by 1977 a generation had moved on and although the party led to New Zealand by Phil Bennett was strong in the forwards, the backs were weak and the All Blacks took their revenge for '71, winning the series 3-1. They did it by playing an expansive game and by running the ball.

Bill Beaumont led England to a Grand Slam in 1980 – their first since 1957 – and ended up as skipper of the Lions who went to South Africa and were beaten in three of the four Tests, but there was never more than seven points between the sides in any of the games.

It was not quite like that three years on. In 1983 Ciaran FitzGerald's Lions went to New Zealand where they were ripped to shreds, losing all four Tests and the last one by an embarrassing 38-6. It was like a return to the dark ages, the old days of the 1960s.

Respect was restored when Scotland's feisty captain Finlay Calder took the Lions on their first three-match series in Australia in 1989 and beat the soon-to-be crowned champions of the world 2-1. Then in 1993 Gavin Hastings' Lions lost a thrilling series in New Zealand 2-1.

The Lions overall record is still more games lost than won, but their brand of rugby, their commitment and their style has always won friends and impressed the world. And only by bringing together the English, Irish, Scots and Welsh can the hegemony of the south be challenged and beaten by the north – Johnson's merry band of men proved that emphatically.

FIFTEEN

The Complete Record

OVERALL RECORD

	P	W	D	L	For	Against
Lions 97	13	11	0	2	480	278

POINTS SCORED: Tries: 56, Conversions: 40, Penalties: 38 Drop Goals: 2
POINTS CONCEDED: Tries: 32; Conversions: 20; Penalties: 26

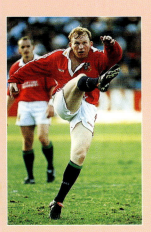

Neil Jenkins broke the century mark with his boot

LIONS LEADING POINTS SCORERS

Tim Stimpson – 111 (4 tries, 23 conversions, 15 penalties)
Neil Jenkins – 110 (2 tries, 17 conversions, 22 penalties)
Tony Underwood – 35 (7 tries); John Bentley – 35 (7 tries)

LIONS LEADING TRY SCORERS

7 Tony Underwood, John Bentley
4 Tim Stimpson, Nick Beal, Jeremy Guscott, Rob Wainwright
3 Ieuan Evans, Matt Dawson
2 Alan Tait, Gregor Townsend, Mike Catt, Mark Regan, Simon Shaw
1 Allan Bateman, Will Greenwood, Kyran Bracken, Austin Healey, Graham Rowntree, Doddie Weir, Neil Back, Lawrence Dallaglio

Tony Underwood breaks free to score one of his seven tour tries

LIONS DROP GOAL SCORERS

1 Jeremy Guscott, Gregor Townsend

SIDELIONS

■ The player who spent the shortest time on the pitch during the tour was Kyran Bracken, who played for just 53 minutes in his one appearance, against Northern Free State.
■ Only seven men played the full 80 minutes in all three Tests. They were: Dallaglio, Dawson, Johnson, Davidson, Gibbs, Wallace and Jenkins.
■ The longest run of consecutive appearances was four by flanker Neil Back.
■ A total of 19 players won their first Lions cap on the tour.
■ The Lions averaged 36.9 points and 4.3 tries per match.

At a Glance – Every Fact From Every Match

	E Prov		Border		W Prov		Mpumalanga		N Transvaal		Gauteng	
Score [Lions first]	39-11		18-14		38-21		64-14		30-36		20-14	
Date	24 May		28 May		31 May		3 June		7 June		11 June	
Back			80				80				80	
Bateman			80				80					
Beal	80						80	T			80	
Bentley			80	T	80	2T			58		80	T
Catt											80	P
Dallaglio	80				80				80			
Davidson	3		80				80				80	
Dawson			25				80	T				
Diprose (R)												
Evans	67				80	T	80	2T				
Gibbs			46						22			
Greenwood	80	T			6		80				80	
Guscott	80	2T			80				80	2T	80	
Healey			55								80	T
Hill	80				80							
Howley	80				80				80			
Jenkins	80	4c2P					80	T7c			22	2c1P
Johnson					80(c)				80(c)			
Leonard	80(c)				80				75			
Miller			80						80			
Quinnell	80				17				80			
Redman (R)											80	
Regan			80	T			28		80			
Rodber					63		80(c)				80(c)	
Rowntree			80		80				80			
Shaw	77				80		14		80			
Smith	80						80				30	
Stimpson			80	P	80	3c4P			80	3c3P		
Tait			34		74	T			80			
Townsend	80				80				80	T		
Underwood	13	T	80				80	2T	80		58	
Wainwright			80(c)	T			80	3T			80	
Wallace			11				73				80	
Weir	80	T	80				66					
Williams	13				80						80	
Wood	67						52					
Young			69				7		5			

Also played: Kyran Bracken (53 mins v N Free State, T), Paul Grayson (80 mins v Border), Tony Stanger (80 mins v N Free State

Natal 42-12 14 June		Em Sboks 51-22 17 June		1st Test 25-16 21 June		Free St 52-30 24 June		2nd Test 18-15 28 June		N FrSt 67-39 1 July		3rd Test 16-35 6 July		Pts	
		80				80		23		80	T	80		5	Back
66		80				80	T			80		40		5	Bateman
		80	3T							80				20	Beal
		80				80	3T	80				80		35	Bentley
14	T	80	T			80				80		80		13	Catt
80	T			80				80				80		5	Dallaglio
		80		80				80				80		0	Davidson
68				80	T			80				79	T	15	Dawson
		80								80				0	Diprose (R)
80				80										15	Evans
80				80				80				80		0	Gibbs
		80				40								5	Greenwood
				80				80	dg			40		23	Guscott
		80				80		3		27		1		5	Healey
80				80				57						0	Hill
12														0	Howley
80	3c6P			80	5P	40	T	80	5P			80	C3P	110	Jenkins
71(c)				80(c)				80(c)				80(c)		0	Johnson
12		80(c)		1		10				39(c)				0	Leonard
80						80		2						0	Miller
														0	Quinnell
		80				80(c)				80				0	Redman (R)
		80								80	T	80		10	Regan
				80				78						0	Rodber
		80	T			70				41				5	Rowntree
80						80				80	2T			10	Shaw
68				79				80				80		0	Smith
		80	T,6c3P			80	T,4c3P			80	2T,7cP	50		111	Stimpson
80				80	T			77						10	Tait
80	T, DG			80				80						13	Townsend
						80	T			80	3T	30		35	Underwood
9		80				80				80		80		20	Wainwright
				80				80				80		0	Wallace
														5	Weir
						80								0	Williams
80				80				80						0	Wood
80						80				80				0	Young

Key: T– Try; c – Conversion; dg – Drop goal; P – Penalty

The Complete Record

LIONS SQUAD, APPEARANCES, POINTS:

Back, Neil Anthony
Height: 5ft 10in Weight: 14st 6lb
Nationality: England. Caps: 5
Lions Caps: 2
Club: Leicester
Position: Flanker
LIONS 97: 7 full appearances / 1 substitute or substituted appearance (583 mins total playing time)

Bateman, Allan Glen
Height: 5ft 9in. Weight: 13st
Nationality: Wales. Caps: 9
Lions Caps: 1
Club: Richmond
Position: Centre
LIONS 97: 5/2 (506 mins)

Beal, Nicholas David
Height: 6ft 2in. Weight: 13st 8lb
Nationality: England. Caps: 1
Lions Caps: 0
Club: Northampton
Position: Wing
LIONS 97: 5/0 (400 mins)

Bentley, John
Height: 6ft. Weight: 15st 7lb
Nationality: England. Caps: 2
Lions Caps: 2
Club: Newcastle
Position: Wing
LIONS 97: 7/1 (618 mins)

Dallaglio, Lawrence Bruno
Height: 6ft 4in
Weight: 16st 5lb
Nationality: England. Caps: 11
Lions Caps: 3
Club: Wasps
Position: Flanker
LIONS 97: 7/0 (560 mins)

Davidson, Jeremy William
Height: 6ft 6in. Weight: 18st
Nationality: Ireland. Caps: 12
Lions Caps: 3
Club: London Irish
Position: Lock
LIONS 97: 7/1 (563 mins)

Dawson, Matthew James Sutherland
Height: 5ft 11in. Weight: 13st
Nationality: England. Caps: 5
Lions Caps: 3
Club: Northampton
Position: Scrum-half
LIONS 97: 3/3 (412 mins)

Evans, Ieuan
Height: 5ft 9in. Weight: 13st 10lb
Nationality: Wales. Caps: 71
Lions Caps: 7
Club: Llanelli
Position: Wing
LIONS 97: 4/1 (387 mins)

Gibbs, Ian Scott
Height: 5ft 10in. Weight: 15st 7lb
Nationality: Wales. Caps: 27
Lions Caps: 5
Club: Swansea
Position: Centre
LIONS 97: 4/2 (388 mins)

Grayson, Paul James
Height: 6ft. Weight: 12st 10lb
Nationality: England. Caps: 8
Lions Caps: 0
Club: Northampton
Position: Fly-half
LIONS 97: 1/0 (80 mins)

Greenwood, William John Heaton
Height: 6ft 3in. Weight: 15st
Nationality: England. Caps: 0
Lions Caps: 0
Club: Leicester
Position: Centre
LIONS 97: 4/2 (366 mins)

Guscott, Jeremy Clayton
Height: 6ft 1in. Weight: 13st 9lb
Nationality: English. Caps: 48
Lions Caps: 8
Club: Bath
Position: Centre
LIONS 97: 6/1 (520 mins)

Healey, Austin
Height: 5ft 10in. Weight: 13st 7lb
Nationality: England. Caps: 2
Lions Caps: 2
Club: Leicester
Position: Scrum-half
LIONS 97: 3/4 (326 mins)

Hill, Richard Anthony
Height: 6ft 3in. Weight: 15st 13lb
Nationality: England. Caps: 4
Lions Caps: 2
Club: Saracens
Position: Flanker
LIONS 97: 4/1 (377 mins)

Howley, Robert
Height: 5ft 9in. Weight: 13st
Nationality: Wales. Caps: 16

Nick Beal charges through to score against Mpumalanga, one of four tries for the Northampton wing on tour

John Bentley gets kitted out for training. He played seven games and won two Lions caps

Lions Caps: 0
Club: Cardiff
Position: Scrum-half
LIONS 97: 3/1 (252 mins)

Jenkins, Neil Roger
Height: 5ft 9in. Weight: 13st 13lb
Nationality: Wales. Caps: 50
Lions Caps: 3
Club: Pontypridd
Position: Fly-half/full-back
LIONS 97: 6/2 (542 mins)

Johnson, Martin Osborne
Height: 6ft 7in. Weight: 17st 12lb
Nationality: England. Caps: 30
Lions Caps: 5
Club: Leicester
Position: Lock
LIONS 97: 5/1 (471 mins)

Leonard, Jason
Height: 5ft 10in. Weight: 17st 7lb
Nationality: England. Caps: 55
Lions Caps: 3
Club: NEC Harlequins
Position: Prop
LIONS 97: 3/5 (377 mins)

Miller, Eric Roger Patrick
Height: 6ft 3in. Weight: 15st 7lb
Nationality: Ireland. Caps: 4
Lions Caps: 1
Club: Leicester
Position: No.8
LIONS 97: 4/1 (322 mins)

Quinnell, Leon Scott
Height: 6ft 4in. Weight: 19st 4lb
Nationality: Wales. Caps: 14
Lions Caps: 0
Club: Richmond
Position: No.8
LIONS 97: 2/1 (177 mins)

Regan, Mark Peter
Height: 5ft 11in. Weight: 18st
Nationality: England. Caps: 12
Lions Caps: 1
Club: Bristol
Position: Hooker
LIONS 97: 5/1 (428 mins)

Rodber, Timothy Andrew Keith
Height: 6ft 6in. Weight: 18st
Nationality: England. Caps: 31
Lions Caps: 2
Club: Northampton & Army
Position: No.8
LIONS 97: 3/2 (381 mins)

Tim Stimpson in rampant mood against the Emerging Springboks

Rowntree, Graham Christopher
Height: 6ft. Weight: 17st 7lb
Nationality: England. Caps: 14
Lions Caps: 0
Club: Leicester
Position: Prop
LIONS 97: 4/2 (431 mins)

Shaw, Simon Dalton
Height: 6ft 9in. Weight: 19st 8lb
Nationality: England. Caps: 6
Lions Caps: 0
Club: Bristol
Position: Lock
LIONS 97: 5/2 (491 mins)

Smith, Thomas James
Height: 5ft 10in. Weight: 17st 4lb
Nationality: Scotland. Caps: 3
Lions Caps: 3
Club: Watsonians
Position: Prop
LIONS 97: 5/2 (547 mins)

Stimpson, Tim Richard George
Height: 6ft 3in. Weight: 15st 7lb
Nationality: England. Caps: 5
Lions Caps: 1
Club: Newcastle
Position: Full-back
LIONS 97: 6/1 (530 mins)

Tait, Alan Victor
Height: 6ft. Weight: 14st
Nationality: Scotland. Caps: 9
Lions Caps: 2
Club: Newcastle
Position: Centre
LIONS 97: 3/3 (425 mins)

Townsend, Gregor Peter John
Height: 6ft. Weight: 13st 12lb
Nationality: Scotland. Caps: 24
Lions Caps: 2
Club: Northampton
Position: Fly-half
LIONS 97: 6/0 (480 mins)

Underwood, Tony
Height: 5ft 9in. Weight 13st 7lb
Nationality: England. Caps: 25
Lions Caps: 1
Club: Newcastle
Position: Wing
LIONS 97: 5/3 (501 mins)

Wainwright, Robert Ian
Height: 6ft 4in. Weight: 15st 7lb
Nationality: Scotland. Caps: 28
Lions Caps: 1

The Lions forwards work out against an imposing backdrop

Martin Johnson rallies his troops. There was never any such thing as an easy game

Club: Watsonians
Position: No.8/Flanker
LIONS 97: 7/1 (569 mins)

Wallace, Paul Stephen
Height: 6ft 1in. Weight: 16st
Nationality. Ireland. 12
Lions Caps: 3
Club: Saracens
Position: Prop
LIONS 97: 4/2 (404 mins)

Weir, George Wilson
Height: 6ft 7in. Weight: 17st 4lb
Nationality: Scotland. Caps: 45
Lions Caps: 0
Club: Newcastle
Position: Second row
LIONS 97: 2/1 (226 mins)

Williams, Barry
Height: 5ft 11in. Weight: 16st 6lb
Nationality: Wales. Caps: 1
Lions Caps: 0
Club: Richmond
Position: Hooker
LIONS 97: 3/1 (253 mins)

Wood, Keith Gerard Mallinson
Height: 6ft. Weight: 16st 5lb
Nationality: Ireland. Caps: 9
Lions Caps: 2
Club: Harlequins
Position: Hooker
LIONS 97: 3/2 (359 mins)

Keith Wood on the
burst, fronted by Joost
van der Westhuizen

Young, David
Height: 6ft 2in. Weight: 18st 7lb
Nationality: Wales. Caps: 21
Lions Caps: 3
Club: Cardiff
Position: Prop
LIONS 97: 3/3 (321 mins)

REPLACEMENTS
Stanger, Tony George
Height: 6ft 2in. Weight: 15st 2lb
Nationality: Scotland. Caps:44
Lions Caps: 0
Club: Hawick
Position: Wing
LIONS 97: 1/0 (80 mins)

Catt, Michael John
Height: 5ft 10. Weight: 13st 2lb
Nationality: England. Caps: 22
Lions Caps: 1
Club: Bath
Position: Fly-half
LIONS 97: 5/1 (414 mins)

Bracken, Kyran Paul Patrick
Height: 5ft 11in. Weight: 12st 9lb
Nationality: England Caps: 13
Lions Caps: 0
Club: Saracens
Position: Scrum-half
LIONS 97: 0/1 (53 mins)

Diprose, Tony
Height: 6ft 5in. Weight: 16st 10lb
Nationality: England. Caps: 2
Lions Caps: 0
Club: Saracens
Position: No.8
LIONS 97: 2/0 (160 mins)

Redman, Nigel
Height: 6ft 4in. Weight: 17st 2lb
Nationality: England. Caps: 19
Lions Caps: 0
Club: Bath
Position: Second row
LIONS 97: 4/0 (320 mins)

Team Manager
Cotton, Francis Edward
Nationality: England
England Caps: 31
Lions Caps: 7

Head Coach
McGeechan, Ian Robert
Nationality: Scotland
Scotland Caps: 32
Lions Caps: 8

Assistant Coach
Telfer, James William
Nationality: Scotland
Scotland Caps: 25
Lions Caps: 8

BACKROOM STAFF
Technical Coaching Assistant
Keast, Andrew Paul
Fitness Adviser – McLean, Dave Alister
Medical Officer – Robson, Dr.James
Physiotherapist – Davies, Mark
Masseur – Wegrzyk, Richard
Baggage Master – Bagshaw, Stanley
Media Liaison Officer – Burrows, Bob
Administrative assistant
Peters, Samantha

Lions fans were quick
to show their true
colours

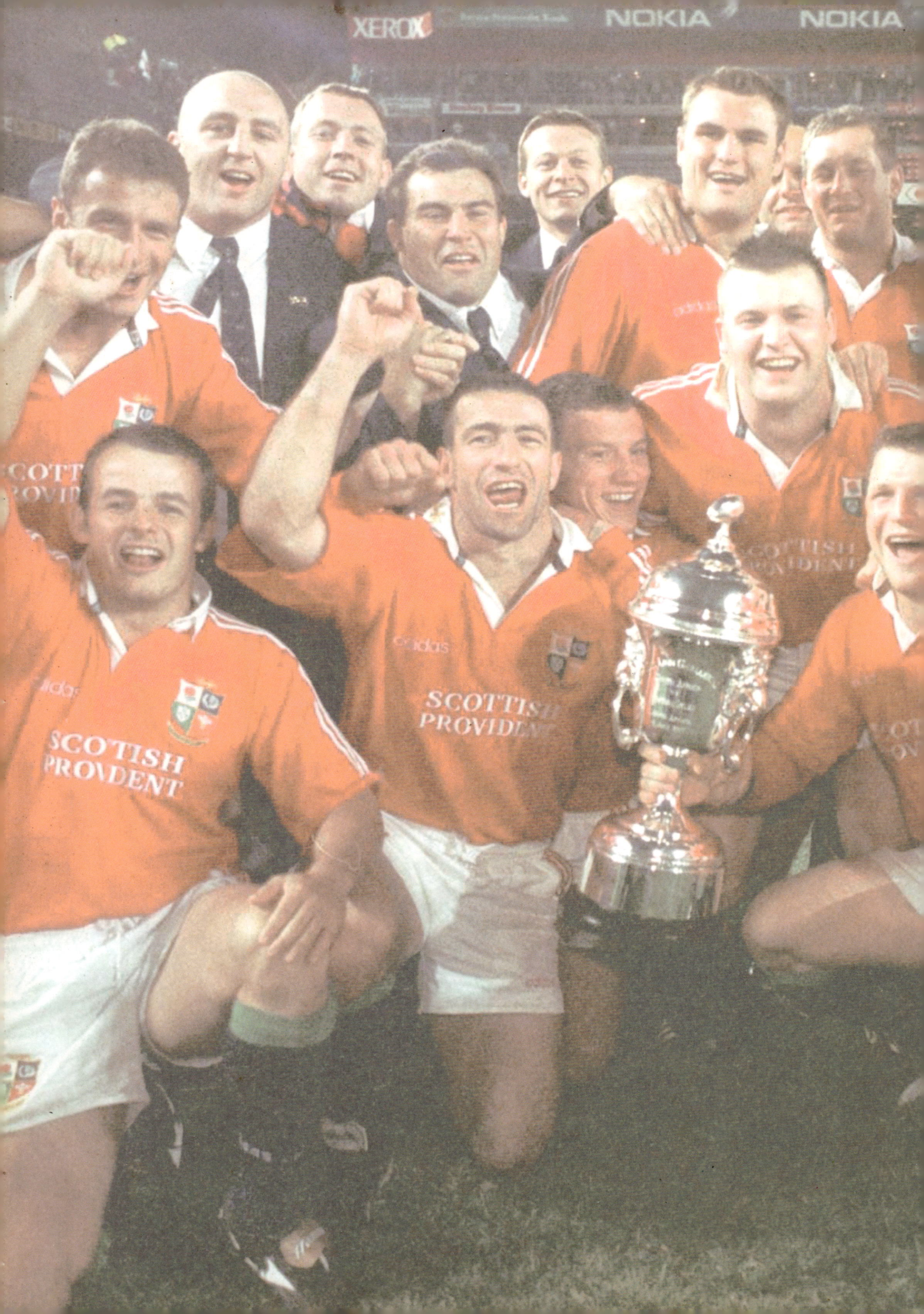
XEROX
NOKIA
NOKIA
adidas
SCOTTISH
PROVIDENT